THE
RACE
OF MY LIFE

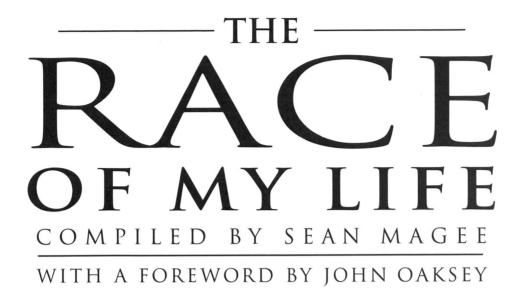

COMPILED BY SEAN MAGEE

WITH A FOREWORD BY JOHN OAKSEY

HEADLINE

First published in 1996
by HEADLINE BOOK PUBLISHING

10 9 8 7 6 5 4 3 2 1

British Library Cataloguing in Publication Data

Race of My Life
I. Magee, Sean
798.400922

ISBN 0-7472-1259-7 (hardback)
0-7472-7778-8 (softback)

Frontispiece: Richard Dunwoody and Miinnehoma, Aintree 1994.

Illustrations
Allsport: p. 1; Carolina Cup Racing Association: p. 54; Chris Cole/Allsport:
pp. 47, colour section v; Gerry Cranham: 16, 26, 31, 32, 36, 38–9, 41, 50, 53, 64,
71, 77, 83, 93, 97, 110, 120, 125, 137, 143, 156, 160, 164, colour section vi (lower), vii;
Tony Edenden/Sportsphoto: pp. 11, 20, 87, 115, colour section iii; David Gadd/
Sportsphoto: p. 14; Trevor Jones: pp. 88, 129, colour section i; Stewart Kendall/
Sportsphoto: pp. 91, 132; New York Racing Association: p. 74; Caroline Norris:
p. 123; Popperfoto: p. 167, colour section ii (lower); Press Association: p. 107;
Gary M. Prior/Allsport: colour section p. viii; David Rogers/Allsport: p. 149;
S&G Press Agency: pp. 58, 104, 112; George Selwyn: pp. 3, 22, 28–9, 43, 60, 78–9,
85, 101, 116, 135, 141, 146, 152, 158, 163, colour section ii (upper), iv (upper and
lower), vi (upper); Chris Smith/Camera Press: pp. 66–7; Mark Thompson/
Popperfoto: frontispiece.

Designed by Charlie Webster at Production Line.

Printed and bound in Great Britain by
BPC Consumer Books Ltd.

HEADLINE BOOK PUBLISHING
A division of Hodder Headline PLC
338 Euston Road
London NW1 3BH

Contents

Preface

'Is it the horse or is it the jockey?' Thus a novice racegoer, grappling with the basics of the sport, cut admirably to the essence of racing as an athletic contest. The answer, of course, is neither alone: the best-bred racehorse is not a great deal of use without a rider, nor does the jockey have much purpose without a mount. You think of the great racehorses and their regular partners as one: Arkle and Pat Taaffe, Brigadier Gerard and Joe Mercer, Mill Reef and Geoff Lewis, Affirmed and Steve Cauthen. Horse and jockey are fused to form the racing machine.

For this book thirty top jockeys – past and present, Flat and National Hunt – were invited to offer accounts of those events which meant most to them in their riding careers, and the text which follows is not 'ghosted' but written up from extensive conversations with them (though a version of Richard Dunwoody's account of the 1994 Grand National has appeared in his book *Duel*, published by Partridge Press). Into the net were trawled every champion jockey on the Flat in Britain since 1964 (Lester Piggott, Willie Carson, Pat Eddery, Joe Mercer, Steve Cauthen, Michael Roberts and Frankie Dettori) and every jumps champion since the 1972–3 season (Ron Barry, Tommy Stack, John Francome, Jonjo O'Neill, Peter Scudamore, Richard Dunwoody and Tony McCoy) in addition to other riders who have graced or are currently gracing the sport. All thirty freely gave their time and memories, and I extend to them all my very grateful thanks – not only for their willingness to participate, but for the many race-riding hints which their pieces contain. In the admittedly unlikely event of my being booked for the Arc, I will now know *never* to make my move until the final straight.

Thanks also to Robert Cooper, who undertook several of the interviews; to Gillian Bromley, long-suffering editor; to Charlie Webster, for his design and type-setting wizardry; to Ron and Audrey Costley, for a safe haven; to Hope Cooper at the Carolina Cup Racing Association; to Phillip Jones; to Tony Sweeney; to John Randall; and to the proprietors of various hostelries around the country who sustained the research phase of this book. At Headline, Alan Brooke showed the consummate patience, stoicism and equanimity which only a lifetime's backing horses can imbue. Celia Kent undertook some fierce schooling early in the campaign but then handed the reins to Lorraine Jerram, who managed to keep her charge – off the bridle even in the parade ring and travelling well within himself only after passing the post – up to his work while staying *just* within the whip guidelines.

Is it the horse or is it the jockey? I hope *The Race of My Life* will illuminate the jockeys' side of the combination. The horses were not available for interview.

S.M.

Foreword by John Oaksey

The Trustees of the Injured Jockeys Fund are deeply grateful to Sean Magee and to all the jockeys who have helped him produce this unique anthology. For once, I honestly don't believe that the word 'unique' is much of an exaggeration. Never before, surely, have so many fine riders chosen and described between two covers the race which retains the strongest hold on their memory, or for which they would most like to be remembered.

Besides extracting the riders' personal accounts, Sean has provided potted biographies of his subjects. They, like the stories, are full of fascinating titbits. Did you know, for instance, that Jason Weaver's father was a professional footballer, that Granville Again regularly ran away with Peter Scudamore at home – or that, after schooling Dawn Run over fences for the first time, Jonjo O'Neill dismissed the Champion Hurdler as 'desperate – couldn't jump a twig . . .'?

Three of my favourite pieces are David Nicholson's account of Mill House's Whitbread, Josh Gifford's various Schweppes Gold Trophy experiences, and Steve Cauthen's epic of the Belmont in which he and Affirmed beat Alydar. Those were the days, all right . . .

Sean and his thirty co-storytellers have been kind enough to give the royalties to the Injured Jockeys Fund; so here is a very brief account of how the money will be spent.

The Fund was founded in 1964 after Paddy Farrell and Tim Brookshaw, two highly successful National Hunt jockeys, suffered injuries which left them paralysed. There was, at that time, no adequate official system of insurance or compensation and the Farrell Brookshaw Appeal, launched by two prominent jumping owners, Edward Courage and Clifford Nicholson, was an immediate success. It was at Paddy and Tim's own unsolicited suggestion that the Fund was thrown open, first to all National Hunt jockeys and a little later to any jockey, professional or amateur, jumping or Flat, provided only that he or she had been licensed or permitted to ride under the Rules of Racing.

There has never been any time limit to the Fund's assistance. It exists to provide help, financial and otherwise, for jockeys and their dependants whose lives have been affected by injuries connected with racing. The nine Trustees, who, with the help of a solicitor Secretary and four paid almoners, control and direct the Fund, are not bound by the terms of any insurance policy. Within certain guidelines developed over the years they have complete discretion. The help they offer already takes many forms, and if new ones are required they will, as far as resources allow, be made available.

In the thirty-two years of its existence, the IJF has received about £3.9 million in donations. It has paid out £3.8 million in grants and assistance to a total of 647 beneficiaries and has £2.3 million outstanding in loans – almost all of them interest-free – to injured jockeys and dependants. So, as those who dismiss the IJF as 'too rich to need any more support' may care to note, *all* the money sent in by our public supporters has been paid out to beneficiaries. Between £6,000 and £7,000 goes out each week in periodic grants, and during last year a total of £382,443 was paid out in financial assistance – still far more than the £186,259 of interest earned by our portfolio of invested capital.

Two recent innovations have been JETS, the Jockeys' Employment and Retraining Scheme, and the holiday on which, for the past three years, a party of beneficiaries, almoners and other helpers have enjoyed ten days of sunshine, warm water and companionship in a specially adapted hotel in Tenerife. JETS, which is partly funded by the Jockeys' Association, is an attempt to solve two of the commonest problems the IJF has faced ever since its foundation. One is the difficulty of persuading jockeys to acquire outside-racing qualifications while still riding; the other, to find them a suitable occupation when they give up. The JETS team at Pollardstown, Elain and Dana Mellor, Sandy Thwaites and Richard Mackaness, have already interviewed over forty candidates and found employment or retraining for twenty-eight.

Whether or not any of Sean Magee's collaborators ever need to have recourse to the Injured Jockeys Fund, they can rest assured that when the royalties from their splendid book come to be spent, the welfare of jockeys will be the first objective.

Lester Piggott

Royal Academy in the Breeders' Cup Mile, Belmont Park, New York, 27 October 1990

Lester Piggott's announcement in September 1995 that he would not be seeking to renew his licence to ride in Britain occasioned little surprise – he was, after all, not far off his sixtieth birthday – but brought to a formal end what was without question the most remarkable career in the history of race-riding. Piggott, eleven times champion jockey, had been at the top of his trade for over forty years, had won big races all around the world, and in his style, achievement, skill, demeanour and personality had left an indelible mark on the Turf.

That his fellow riders gave him a tumultuous standing ovation as well as a special award at the Jockeys' Association dinner in London in March 1996, almost a year and a half after he had last ridden in a race in Britain, was just another indication of the extraordinary charisma which Piggott – variously nicknamed 'The Long Fellow' or 'The Maestro' but universally known and revered simply as Lester – possessed for all who came into contact with him. As he went up to receive his award that evening the speakers blared forth (predictably) the Tina Turner song whose title told in three words the Lester Piggott story: 'Simply The Best'.

Born in Wantage on 5 November 1935, Lester Piggott was bred to be a jockey. His grandfather Ernie was champion National Hunt rider three times and partnered three Grand National winners; his father Keith was a jockey and trainer, who in 1963 would send out Grand National winner Ayala; his mother was a member of the famous jockey-producing Rickaby dynasty.

Young Lester had his first ride in public on a filly named The Chase at Salisbury on 7 April 1948, and at Haydock Park on 18 August the same year rode his first winner on the same filly in the Wigan Lane Selling Handicap. She was three years old; he was twelve. Over a year passed before he scored his second win, but then his career found a true turn of foot. In 1950 and 1951 he was champion apprentice, in 1952 he came second in the Derby on Gay Time (and fell off the colt just after passing the post behind Tulyar), and in 1954 he had his first success in an English Classic at the age of eighteen, when 33–1 shot Never Say Die made him the youngest jockey to win the Derby this century.

In all he won the Derby nine times – Never Say Die's victory being emulated by Crepello (1957), St Paddy (1960), Sir Ivor (1968), Nijinsky (1970), Roberto (1972), Empery (1976), The Minstrel (1977) and Teenoso (1983) – among a record thirty English Classics: in addition to those nine Derbies, the One Thousand Guineas twice, Two Thousand Guineas five times, Oaks six times and St Leger eight times. Nine of those thirty Classic wins were on horses trained in Ireland by Vincent O'Brien, whose partnership with Piggott was the stuff of racing legend.

Piggott won seven French Classics, sixteen Irish Classics and countless other big races in Europe, including the King George VI and Queen Elizabeth Stakes seven times and the Prix de l'Arc de Triomphe three times. He rode winners all over the world, and by the end of his career had won 4,493 on the Flat in Britain, plus twenty over hurdles (he won the Triumph Hurdle on Prince Charlemagne in 1954). His career total placed him second to Gordon Richards (with 4,870 winners) in the all-time list of British-based Flat jockeys, but the addition of his overseas haul (over 800 races) takes him well past Richards.

Much more important than the statistics are the horses with whom Piggott was associated – including, apart from those nine Derby winners, the likes of Gladness, Petite Etoile, Dahlia, Alleged, Moorestyle, Park Top, Ardross, Sagaro, Meadow Court, Commanche Run, Rodrigo De Triano and so many more.

In 1985 he retired from the saddle to take up training at the yard he had built in Newmarket many years before, and in 1986, his first year as a trainer, sent out thirty winners, including Cutting Blade in the Coventry Stakes at Royal Ascot.

If Piggott was a phenomenon on the racecourse, off it he tended to cut an enigmatic and remote figure, whose carefulness with money had been the stuff of Turf lore for decades. Even so, news that he was being investigated for tax fraud alarmed the racing world – and sent some other leading jockeys scurrying off for emergency meetings with their accountants – and his conviction and imprisonment in October 1987 sent shock waves round the sport. Released on parole in October 1988, Piggott spent a quiet couple of years rehabilitating himself before stunning racing with a return to the saddle in October 1990, three weeks short of his fifty-fifth birthday. Beaten a short head on his return ride at Leicester, he rode the first winner of his 'new' career at Chepstow on his second day back – Nicholas, trained by his wife Susan – and at the end of the following week crowned one of the most remarkable stories in sporting history with what has to be, despite so much fierce competition, the race of his life.

66 Vincent O'Brien had been very instrumental in my decision to return to the saddle. In spring 1990 I had gone across to Ballydoyle to ride work for him, and later had asked if he could supply me with a ride for a veterans' race at The Curragh in July. He came up with Legal Legend – on whom I'd ridden work on the earlier occasion – and we finished third: a far cry from the Derby or Arc, maybe, but it was still wonderful to be teaming up with Vincent again.

A few weeks after that I was on the phone to Vincent when he said, quite out of the blue: 'Why don't you make a comeback?' I promised to think about it, but it was only after a lunch with him at the Berkeley Court Hotel in Dublin in September 1990 that the idea started to take serious shape. At the time his stable jockey was John Reid, but their agreement was due to terminate at the end of 1990, and Vincent undertook that if I did decide to return to the saddle he'd give me first choice of mounts on his horses in 1991. He was by then operating on a much smaller scale than in his heyday, but the watchword with him was – as always – quality, and I knew that first choice for Ballydoyle would mean some plum rides. This made the whole idea of a comeback very tempting. I decided to go ahead – and in the event the link-up with Vincent came about much sooner than we'd anticipated.

John Reid (who had partnered Royal Academy in all his previous races) was due to ride a funny old sprinter called Whippet in the Prix de l'Abbaye at Longchamp on Arc day (at which point my plan for a comeback was still being kept very firmly under wraps), and as the horses were being loaded into the stalls the horse jinked and dumped John on the ground. It looked a fairly innocuous fall at the time but John broke a collarbone and was out of action as the Breeders' Cup at Belmont Park approached.

Lester Piggott and Royal Academy collar Itsallgreektome.

After John had been sidelined I'd met Vincent at the Tattersalls Sales in Newmarket and mentioned to him that I'd be happy to ride Royal Academy in the Breeders' Cup Mile. Unsurprisingly, he'd had other offers, but after consulting the board of Classic Thoroughbreds – the top-of-the-range syndicate which had the majority share in the colt – agreed that I could take the ride.

The omens earlier in the week of the race were good. On the Tuesday I went across to The Curragh and rode four horses for Vincent. All won. Two days later, after riding in the last at Newbury, I headed off for Heathrow to catch Concorde to New York. I checked into the Waldorf Astoria, where I met Vincent's wife Jacqueline and son Charles: sadly Vincent himself had flu and could not travel over for the race. I myself had a cold, a condition which tended to make me two or three pounds heavier than usual, and I had to be very careful what I ate in the couple of days before the Breeders' Cup.

'I was never one to think too much about past races'

On the Friday I had to undertake formalities such as passing my medical and obtaining a jockey's licence – which set me back $300 – as well as making the acquaintance of Royal Academy, whom I had not sat on before, taking him for a gentle canter around the Belmont Park training track. A big, very good-looking son of my old partner Nijinsky, he impressed me as a horse of great quality, though there were – as with other Nijinsky horses – question marks against his temperament: I'd seen all his races, and it seemed to me that he tended not to apply himself as hard as he might. As a two-year-old he'd won on his first outing before flopping badly in the Dewhurst Stakes at Newmarket – perhaps he just wasn't ready for a race of that stature – then at three had shown plenty of high-class form. After winning over seven furlongs at The Curragh he was narrowly beaten by Tirol in the Irish Two Thousand Guineas, then blotted his copybook badly when refusing to go into the starting stalls before the St James's Palace Stakes at Royal Ascot. He then reverted to sprinting, and suspicions that his temperament was getting the better of him were allayed when he gave no trouble before the July Cup at Newmarket, which he won well. I thought he'd been a little unlucky when second to Dayjur in the Ladbroke Sprint Cup at Haydock Park, his last race before America.

The original intention had been to run Royal Academy in the Challenge Stakes at Newmarket in mid-October, but Vincent decided to aim him at the bigger prize – the Breeders' Cup Mile was worth $1 million – and he merited his place in the line-up alongside other good European milers like Markofdistinction and Priolo and the American horse Steinlen, who had been runner-up to Miesque in the Mile in 1988 and won it in 1989. For all the strength of the opposition, Royal Academy started favourite.

I walked the track before racing and was surprised to find how rough the turf course was, but it would be the same for all of us, and I was very confident of a big run from Royal Academy. So, to judge from the reception I had when I got up on the colt in the paddock, was the large contingent of British and Irish racegoers who had made the trip. By the time of the Mile that Breeders' Cup day had already produced plenty of sensation, with Dayjur jumping a shadow on the track when he had the Sprint at his mercy,

Breeders' Cup Mile

Belmont Park, New York, 27 October 1990   *1 mile*

1	ROYAL ACADEMY	L. Piggott	5–2 fav
2	Itsallgreektome	C. Nakatani	36–1
3	Priolo	C. Asmussen	9–2

Also ran: Steinlen (4th), Expensive Decision, Who's To Pay, Markofdistinction, Lady Winner, Jalaajel, Go Dutch, Shot Gun Scott, Great Normand, Colway Rally

13 ran   *neck, $\frac{3}{4}$ length*

and the great duel in the Distaff between Go For Wand and Bayakoa, a tussle broken only by the tragic fall of Go For Wand close home.

So the atmosphere was highly charged as we started to make our way out of the paddock – at which point Royal Academy decided to demonstrate his well-being by putting in a huge buck, shooting me out of the saddle but luckily staying underneath me when I came down. I decided to dispense with the outrider who was supposed to accompany us to the start and take him down quietly by himself.

This seemed to settle him, and he gave no trouble going into the stalls, even though as he was drawn on the inside he had to go in first. Waiting for the others to load seemed to help him relax – to the extent that when the stalls opened he was still dozing, and missed the break. In the event this was just as well, as the horse drawn next to him broke fast but was run into the inside rail, interference that Royal Academy did well to miss.

In any case, my plan had been to drop him out and give him every chance of getting the mile – a distance he had not run over since the Irish Two Thousand Guineas back in May – and down the back straight I was content to sit well off the pace, with only three behind me. Going into the final bend I moved him up towards a challenging position, and as we started to straighten up I was beginning to think I'd win, when all of a sudden he lost his action completely. He did not stumble, but seemed to miss a stride – maybe he put his foot in a hole on that rough surface – and in doing so lost his place.

Royal Academy had had problems with his feet and ran in stick-on plastic shoes rather than the conventional nailed-on ones, but it turned out that his losing his action had not been caused by any shoe problem. Whatever the cause of this hiccough, it transformed what we had to do: from holding a good challenging position we were suddenly struggling to get back into the race, and this would be no time for Royal Academy to shirk the issue. I had to get after him with a vengeance, but he really stuck his head out and showed his heart. Itsallgreektome, a grey colt ridden by Corey

Nakatani, took the lead a furlong out and was going hard for the wire, but once Royal Academy had recovered his rhythm he simply flew up the centre of the track. We caught the grey in the final strides and won by a neck.

Jacqueline O'Brien led Royal Academy into the winner's circle and we had a wonderful reception from the crowd. I never used to get very elated, but for once I felt truly on a high. Winning such a prize – the richest of my career – on a horse trained by Vincent O'Brien, with whom I had had so many great moments for over thirty years, made this a very special occasion indeed.

For all that, I was never one to think too much about past races. My attitude was to keep concentrating on the next, not the last.

A race is a race. **"**

Richard Dunwoody

Miinnehoma in the Martell Grand National, Aintree, 9 April 1994

BY THE CLOSE OF THE 1995–6 NATIONAL Hunt season Richard Dunwoody had ridden 1,367 winners over jumps in Great Britain, which total puts him second only to Peter Scudamore (1,678 winners) in the all-time rankings. Champion jockey for the first time in the 1992–3 term, he retained his title the following year after a memorable struggle with Adrian Maguire which went down to the very last fixture of the season at Market Rasen, and came out top again in 1994–5. By then Dunwoody, though barely into his thirties, was an elder statesman of his profession, and to no great surprise announced that he would no longer charge around the country in search of championships, but concentrate on enjoying what would inevitably be the last few seasons of a wonderful career. Away from the pressure-cooker atmosphere of the race for the title, his skills glowed even more brightly, and his association during the 1995–6 term with such horses as One Man and Sound Man saw him at the peak of his powers.

For many observers, those powers are unmatched in the history of riding over fences: a great horseman and supreme stylist, particularly skilled in presenting a horse at a fence to enable it to jump fluently and efficiently, Dunwoody has also raised to new heights the dedication and focus which the modern jockey needs to maintain his place at the top.

Richard Dunwoody was born in Belfast on 18 January 1964, and rode his first pony at the age of two. He had his first ride under Rules in August 1982 and on 4 May 1983 he rode his first winner: Game Trust in a hunter chase at Cheltenham. Within seven years he had joined one of National Hunt racing's greatest elites, jockeys who have won the Champion Hurdle, Cheltenham Gold Cup and Grand National: the treble has been achieved since the war only by Dunwoody, Fred Winter, Willie Robinson and Bobby Beasley. Richard Dunwoody won his first National on West Tip in 1986 (and his second on Miinnehoma eight years later), the Gold Cup on Charter Party in 1988, and the Champion Hurdle on Kribensis in 1990. But the horse with whom he has been most closely connected in the public mind is Desert Orchid, on whom he won seven races, including the King George VI Chase in 1989 and 1990 and the Racing Post Chase and Irish National in 1990.

❝ In the Racing Post Chase at Kempton Park in February 1990 Desert Orchid was the best I ever knew him. He led early on, was headed and then came back to lead again in the straight to go away and win under twelve stone three – a fantastic performance. He probably wasn't quite as good as that in the Irish National at Fairyhouse a couple of months later, but that day is memorable for the greeting which the crowd gave the horse. It was the only time he ran in a steeplechase outside England, and he was practically mobbed. Even before the race the reception was unbelievable, with racegoers crowding into the paddock to try to pull hairs out of his tail.

The race itself mostly went according to plan, until between the last two fences – by which time he was leading and feeling like the winner – he became so tired that he lost his action and seemed to have gone lame. At the last fence he was desperately weary. I tried to get him back on his hocks to jump it but he couldn't put himself right, and made an apparently almighty blunder. In fact it looked much worse than it felt to me, and I never thought he was going to fall. He won by twelve lengths from Barney Burnett, and received a wonderful welcome afterwards.

Naturally my Champion Hurdle and Gold Cup wins were landmarks, but I also cherish a special Cheltenham memory of Rushing Wild in the 1993 Gold Cup. He gave me a superb ride, jumping well all the way round. I kicked on at the top of the hill, and on turning into the straight thought briefly that I might win. Then I saw Mark Dwyer on Jodami looming upsides, and that was that. A great ride none the less.

But the race which gave me most satisfaction has to be Miinnehoma's Grand National in 1994.

I'd first ridden Miinnehoma, who was owned by comedian Freddie Starr and had won the Sun Alliance Chase at Cheltenham in 1992, when schooling him at Martin Pipe's earlier that season, and he then won at Newbury on his first race for over a year; I was grounded with a suspension when he ran unplaced in the Cheltenham Gold Cup. Although an eleven-year-old, he'd run in only seventeen races, had plenty of class, and was a very tidy and efficient jumper, though I'd never really thought of him as a National winner. So I was hopeful rather than expectant, an attitude reflected in the betting market: he started at 16–1, with David Nicholson's Moorcroft Boy, ridden by Adrian Maguire, favourite at 5–1, the good hunter chaser Double Silk 6–1 and Gold Cup winner The Fellow bracketed with Master Oats on 9–1.

The previous year's National had been the non-starting 'Race That Never Was', and various procedures were newly in place to ensure that fiasco was not repeated, but among the jockeys there was no extra tension – just the usual keenness to get on with it.

Miinnehoma had idled with me in his Newbury race and the key to my tactics now was to avoid hitting the front too soon. In any National the best strategy is not to get too far behind, as there are usually loose horses around later in the race who can cause interference, and my plan that year was simple enough: get a good break, stay handy, find a rhythm and keep it until the race got serious on the second circuit.

But everyone's plans had to reckon with one other big factor: the going. The 1994 Grand National was run in conditions so desperate that the day before the race there was even speculation about whether it could take place at all. Torrential rain throughout the Friday had turned the ground very heavy, which would naturally put a premium on stamina and jumping, but as far as Miinnehoma was concerned I had few worries on that score, as he'd shown in the past that he could go on heavy ground.

We had a good start, and though I'd aimed to break handy and settle Miinnehoma in, he ran quite keen going down over the Melling Road towards the first fence, and I had to restrain him. He jumped the first big but well, and the drop on the landing side didn't affect him: he was very sure-footed and soon learned to adapt to the unusual fences.

He popped over the second, then wasn't too clever at the third, the big open ditch. But his mistake there was just what I needed, as it dropped him back through the field a little to where I wanted to be, well off the leaders. He jumped the fourth fine, but by the fifth was a little closer to the inner than I ideally wanted, as the sixth is Becher's Brook, and even since the modifications it can be risky jumping Becher's on the inside where the drop is much more marked than on the outer. Miinnehoma naturally jumps to the left, so approaching Becher's I let him drift out to put himself right, and he met the fence spot-on, finding a very good stride and jumping neatly – though pecking slightly on landing.

'One moment his head was scraping the floor – but the next he was up and galloping again'

He skipped over the seventh nicely and was handily placed in fifth going over the Canal Turn, and as we set off towards Valentine's Brook and the long run towards the stands there was a moment to take stock. Miinnehoma was going well within himself, relaxed and happy. I, on the other hand, was not. In the very big races the surge of adrenalin sometimes causes tension and irregular breathing, and after the Canal Turn I realised that I was too tense for my own or my horse's good. So I made a conscious effort to calm down, to say to myself that everything was going according to plan and I had to relax – keep concentrating but wind down a little. By the time we reached Valentine's I had taken a few deep breaths and was back in my own rhythm.

At Valentine's I became aware of Jamie Osborne on Garrison Savannah coming up the inner, having a great ride. The Fellow was right there, but two after Valentine's I just glimpsed Young Hustler being knocked over by a loose horse. The pace was being set by Double Silk, and I was happy enough to keep my fellow fifth or sixth, getting a good lead and popping away at his fences.

Coming over the Melling Road and turning on to the racecourse proper there seemed to be several loose horses around – the heavy ground had already taken its toll – and I was anxious to avoid trouble at the two fences before the Chair. At the thirteenth, the first after the turn towards home, Double Silk fell heavily just in front of me and I heard a fair bit of crashing all around: I learned later that Master Oats had gone here. We popped over the fourteenth and made for the Chair, the highest and narrowest jump on the course. A loose horse was in front of me, so I aimed to go down the inner, but Garrison Savannah got the inside berth and Miinnehoma jumped the Chair one off – and to my great relief the loose horse ran out.

As we went over the water jump and set out for the second circuit Garrison Savannah was disputing the lead with Riverside Boy, another of Martin Pipe's runners, with Miinnehoma going beautifully in third. But Riverside Boy was beginning to let his temperament get the better of him and didn't fancy another circuit: although Mark Richards managed to persuade him to round the bend by the racecourse stables he was fighting a losing battle, and the horse veered right over to the far rail before refusing at the seventeenth, the first fence second time around.

Going out into the country towards that seventeenth I called across to Jamie Osborne to ask how he was enjoying himself, but he barely had time to reply – very positively – before Garrison Savannah was shoved out of the race by a loose horse when just about to take off.

Miinnehoma had seen this loose horse trying to stop at the fence and himself seemed to feel like easing up, and now my problems were beginning. With grief going on all round me I was in danger of getting to the front much too soon, and my horse needed a lead to stop him backing off his fences. I was having to take a fair pull to get company – and had to roar at Miinnehoma to get him to jump the eighteenth, so reluctant was he becoming. I called across to Adam Kondrat on The Fellow to give me a lead, but he too was trying not to hit the front! Mercifully Ebony Jane and Liam Cusack then appeared on the scene, and we had company.

At the big ditch – the nineteenth – Miinnehoma was in the lead although I did not want him to be, and again I had to shout at him to get him to jump. I knew that if I slacked off he'd start backing away from his fences again, and to my great relief Liam then took it up on Ebony Jane. It was about here that Simon Burrough on Just So – an old battler who needed extreme distances and heavy going to be seen at his best – came alongside, about a mile earlier than I would have expected!

Approaching second Becher's only Ebony Jane was on my outer, and I pulled Miinnehoma out far wider than he'd jumped on the first circuit. I wanted to get away from all those loose horses, who could have run down the fence and hampered him, and I also wanted to minimize the effect of the drop. Things were going so well that there was no point in taking unnecessary risks. He jumped the fence fine but pecked badly on landing, and for a fraction of a second I thought I might have gone. One moment his head was scraping the floor – but the next he was up and galloping again, without any loss of momentum. As we popped over the twenty-third upsides Ebony Jane everything was still going well, but I was beginning to worry about the thinness of the company around us, and was also well aware that Miinnehoma had never been four and a half miles before, and that there might be a limit to his stamina.

At the Canal Turn, Liam and I were joined by Simon Burrough on Just So, and I imagined that one or two were queuing up behind to take us on. The Fellow fell heavily at the Canal Turn, though I didn't see this; nor was

I aware at that stage that Adrian Maguire and Moorcroft Boy were making good progress. At the fifth last we went through a gap in the spruce, and at the final ditch, with Just So on our inner and Ebony Jane on our outer, Miinnehoma was spot on.

I went too long at the third last but my horse fiddled very well. As we made our way back again across the Melling Road and on to the racecourse I glanced round – and there was this chestnut head with a white blaze: Moorcroft Boy. He had been off the bridle, but when he ranged up alongside me he was going very well.

Miinnehoma was still on the bridle, with Just So and Ebony Jane ahead of us and Moorcroft Boy on the outside. But both Ebony Jane and Just So seemed to be struggling, and going to the second last I didn't want to get boxed in and risk getting hampered should one or both of these tired horses make a mistake or fall. So I went for a gap between them, and at the same time Adrian came round the outside.

At the second last Miinnehoma came up long for me, and all the way from that fence to the last I was letting Adrian give me a lead. My fellow was still cantering. He felt as if he'd trot up, but it was vital that he didn't hit the front too soon as I was sure he'd then stop, so I had to sit and suffer.

Richard Dunwoody and Miinnehoma (right) hold off Simon Burrough and Just So.

Martell Grand National

Aintree, 9 April 1994 $4\frac{1}{2}$ miles

1 MIINNEHOMA	R. Dunwoody	16–1
2 Just So	S. Burrough	20–1
3 Moorcroft Boy	A. Maguire	5–1 fav

Also ran: Ebony Jane (4th), Fiddlers Pike, Roc de Prince, Zeta's Lad, Into The Red, Rust Never Sleeps, The Fellow, Mister Ed, Channels Gate, Riverside Boy, Run For Free, Garrison Savannah, Paco's Boy, He Who Dares Wins, Quirinus, Black Humour, Topsham Bay, Double Silk, Mr Boston, Master Oats, Mighty Falcon, Young Hustler, Southern Minstrel, Captain Brandy, Gay Ruffian, Laura's Beau, New Mill House, It's A Cracker, Romany King, Ushers Island, Henry Mann, Elfast, Fourth Of July

36 ran $1\frac{1}{4}$ lengths, 20 lengths

Adrian started to nudge away at Moorcroft Boy – which was not a sight I wanted to see just yet – and a loose horse, which turned out to be Young Hustler, then started to come between us.

Coming to the last, I felt I had the measure of Moorcroft Boy, even though he was just in front of me as we jumped it. Then on landing Adrian quickened away, and for a moment I thought he was going to get home after all. For about ten strides after the last he was definitely getting away from me, and all of a sudden I was off the bridle. So I pulled my whip through and gave Miinnehoma one smack, at which he started to surge forward as Moorcroft Boy came to the end of his tether. This was getting tricky! We were nearly halfway up the run-in but I couldn't put Miinnehoma under pressure as I knew he'd stop in front, so the only thing to do was to take a pull. The loose Young Hustler was still giving me a lead – but for how long?

At the Elbow, halfway up the run-in, Young Hustler veered off towards the stands rail, removing my lead. I started nudging Miinnehoma, to keep him up to his work without putting the gun to his head. As I did so he spooked slightly at some traffic cones in the angle of the Elbow and hesitated for a moment when the tunnel of noise hit him – and then a new threat appeared in the shape of a big black horse's head looming up on my right.

This was Just So, who was in his element in the closing stages of a four-and-a-half-mile race in heavy ground and had rallied after the last, cutting down Moorcroft Boy at the Elbow and for a moment looking sure to go past us. He probably got to within about a neck, but the sight of him spurred Miinnehoma on. I picked up my stick, gave my horse a smack, and he started to run on for it. In the last hundred yards he was drawing away, and at the line won by a length and a quarter from Just So, with Moorcroft Boy twenty lengths further back in third and Ebony Jane a remote fourth. There were only two other finishers.

The rest of the afternoon was a bit of a blur. Freddie Starr was unable to be at Aintree but I spoke with him over the mobile phone during the post-race television interview with Des Lynam, and after numerous other interviews and celebrations I finally got home about two the following morning.

I had to fill in a report form for Martin Pipe after each race I rode for him, and about Miinnehoma I wrote that the horse had idled slightly in front: my recommendation was to leave it a little later next time . . . **"**

Frankie Dettori

Lammtarra in the King George VI and Queen Elizabeth Diamond Stakes, Ascot, 22 July 1995

IT IS DIFFICULT, VERGING ON IMPOSSIBLE, TO describe the effect of Frankie Dettori on the British racing world without at some point resorting to the well-worn phrase 'a breath of fresh air'. Dettori has not been the first young jockey – nor will he be the last – to illuminate the sport with a precocious talent in the saddle and ride big winners at a preposterously early age, but in his case the riding brilliance has been teamed with an exuberance and *joie de vivre*, a simple delight in what he does and an inclination to share that delight with all around him, which has made the ebullient Italian – well, a breath of fresh air.

Many observers have declared Dettori the most exciting young talent to grace Flat racing since Lester Piggott started making a name for himself after riding his first winner at the age of twelve in 1948, and the comparison with Piggott is certainly valid in terms of their backgrounds. Lester was born into a family steeped in racing history (see page 1), and Frankie Dettori had the inestimable benefit of a famous jockey for a father: Gianfranco Dettori, one of the greatest Italian riders of the century (thirteen times champion in his native country) and winner of the Two Thousand Guineas on Bolkonski in 1975 and Wollow in 1976. His son Lanfranco was born in Milan on 15 December 1970, and in 1985 joined trainer Luca Cumani in Newmarket. Too young to ride in races in Britain, Frankie returned to Italy, where at the age of fifteen he rode his first winner, Rif, at Turin on 16 November 1986.

His first British victory came on Lizzy Hare in the Birdless Grove Handicap at Goodwood on 9 June 1987, and he finished that season with eight winners. In 1988 he rode twenty-two winners in Britain, and the following year became champion apprentice with seventy-five, equalling Edward Hide's post-war record. The plum job of stable jockey to Luca Cumani went to Dettori in 1990, and the end of that season saw him in fourth place in the jockeys' table with 141 winners, two of which – Markofdistinction in the Queen Elizabeth II Stakes and Shamshir in the Fillies' Mile on the same afternoon at

Ascot – brought him his first Group One victories in Britain. At nineteen, he was the first teenager to ride over 100 winners in a season since Lester Piggott in 1955.

As Dettori's undoubted talents came to be appreciated more widely, so he was put up on better and better horses, and his association with the great sprinting filly Lochsong in 1993 and 1994 captured the imagination of the racing public. In 1994 he was short-headed in both the One Thousand Guineas and Two Thousand Guineas, then landed his first English Classic on Balanchine in the Oaks, his first Irish Derby on the same filly, and his first Breeders' Cup race when Barathea stormed home in the Mile at Churchill Downs. That same season he made a concerted attack on the jockeys' championship by building up a huge lead on the all-weather tracks in the early months of the year, so that by the time his main rivals got under way late in March he was so far ahead that they had no realistic chance of catching him. His final total was an extraordinary 233 winners, the highest figure achieved by any jockey riding in Britain other than Gordon Richards. The fact that he had ridden in 1,317 races in order to amass that total was a new record for mounts in one season and testimony to his dedication to the task.

He was again champion in 1995, with 211 winners, and that season won two more English Classics – the Oaks on Moonshell and the St Leger on Classic Cliche, which by an act of sublimely good planning was Frankie Dettori's 1,000th winner in Britain.

Yet when the horse who really made 1995 an *annus mirabilis* for Frankie Dettori won the Derby, it was with a rival jockey in the plate …

66 The Derby, the King George VI and Queen Elizabeth Diamond Stakes and the Prix de l'Arc de Triomphe have long been the three races in the world I most wanted to win, and although Lammtarra gave me the huge pleasure of winning the last two, after the 1995 Derby he wasn't exactly my favourite horse.

After being trained as a two-year-old by the late Alex Scott and winning on his only appearance as a juvenile, Lammtarra wintered with the Godolphin team in Dubai, where he'd had a serious problem with an abscess on the lung. He gradually regained his fitness, but when he came back to England in the spring he was not – at least as far as I was concerned – a horse on whom to pin any particular hopes. I knew him to be a very nice colt, but never gave him much thought. In the run-up to the Derby I was aware that he was beginning to work well, but it would be very difficult for a horse to win the Derby on only his second racecourse appearance ever, and first time out as a three-year-old. Obviously Sheikh Mohammed could see some potential in the horse that others couldn't.

Walter Swinburn, who had ridden him on his only outing at two, had the ride in the Derby, and I was on Sheikh Mohammed's Tamure, trained by John Gosden. Inside the final furlong I was busy trying to get my horse past the leader Fahal, and once I had done so thought perhaps for a second that I'd win when – whoosh! – suddenly Lammtarra and Walter appeared out of nowhere and went past us. It was a fantastic performance.

Although I rode plenty of the Godolphin runners, Lammtarra was clearly Walter's ride, and as the King George VI and Queen Elizabeth Diamond Stakes at Ascot approached in late July my probable mount in the race looked like being either Balanchine – on whom I had won the Oaks and Irish

Derby in 1994 but who had severely disappointed us on her four-year-old debut at Royal Ascot – or possibly the 1994 Arc winner Carnegie, trained by André Fabre: Carnegie was coming back to form but would probably be ridden at Ascot by Thierry Jarnet. Balanchine had started to work better but we still weren't sure whether she'd be ready for as important a race as the King George.

I'd been going flat out all year and felt in need of a short break, so with a few quiet days preceding the big Ascot meeting I asked John Gosden whether I could take myself away for a short holiday. He agreed, and I flew off to Sardinia. On the Wednesday before the race I phoned my agent Matty Cowing:

'Hey – what's going on at the weekend?'

Matty said: 'Have you got a chair near you?'

'Yeah.'

**Done it!
Frankie Dettori
and Lammtarra
ease up after beating
Michael Hills and Pentire.**

'Sit down.'

'Right. What's happened?'

'You've got a ride in the King George.'

'Come on, then – who is it?'

'Are you sitting down?'

'Yes, yes!'

'LAMMTARRA!'

I thought Matty was joking, but he wasn't, and although I never knew – and still don't – why Godolphin had decided to drop Walter, who after all had won the Derby on the colt, it was not up to me to find out. On my return I felt glad, however, that I'd been in Sardinia for those few days and had missed all the hype and controversy. I'm a great friend of Walter's – we get changed next to each other – and on seeing him at Ascot on the Friday, the day before the race, told him I just didn't know what to say. He was very good about it, not only wishing me luck but giving me some crucial advice about Lammtarra: the one thing to remember is that when you dig, you'll find; don't give up on him – keep digging, and you'll keep finding.

Jocking off Walter, however innocently, added pressure before the race. If I won it would be said that he would have won as well; if I lost it might be said that he would have won. I was on a hiding to nothing.

I went to see the horse in the morning, though never actually sat on him until being legged up in the parade ring before the race, and walking round the paddock concentrated hard on what I had to do. Lammtarra was a wonderful horse but a little weird, and I knew that he had a reputation at home for getting his own way: if he didn't want to work, he didn't work. He tended to take the mickey, but was so brilliant that they didn't want to risk upsetting him.

He may have won the Derby but he was still a highly inexperienced horse for such a searching test as the King George, the most important mid-season middle-distance race in Europe, and even the most experienced horse can find Ascot a tough and tricky track, with its short run up the home straight. There were only seven runners in the race, but the draw would be crucial, and I was very keen for him to be given an outside berth so that I could drop him in and keep him clear of the trouble which he might have to contend with if drawn on the inner – essential for a horse with little racing experience. Going to the races on the Friday I was praying for an outside draw – and mightily relieved to see on the list in the weighing room that he'd drawn the number two berth, with one of his main dangers Pentire outside him. Great!

Lammtarra was favourite for the race, but was challenged in the betting market by Carnegie and by Pentire, who had gone through the season unbeaten: he had not been thought to be good enough to enter in the Derby, but then had won the Classic Trial at Sandown Park, the Predominate Stakes at Goodwood, the Dee Stakes at Chester, and the King Edward VII Stakes at Royal Ascot. The other four runners were the Irish Derby winner Winged Love, Broadway Flyer, Strategic Choice and old Environment Friend.

King George VI and Queen Elizabeth Diamond Stakes

Ascot, 22 July 1995 $1\frac{1}{2}$ miles

1	LAMMTARRA	L. Dettori	9–4 fav
2	Pentire	M. Hills	3–1
3	Strategic Choice	T. Quinn	25–1

Also ran: Winged Love (4th), Broadway Flyer, Carnegie, Environment Friend

7 ran   neck, $1\frac{1}{2}$ lengths

Lammtarra was very well behaved in the parade before the race and I got a good lead down to the start, but once there he started to fool about. It was a very hot day and I'd wanted him to cool down under the trees by the mile and a half start, but he began to monkey around and refused to keep still. One of the stalls handlers came to help, but Lammtarra continued to try to take me for a joyride, until eventually we managed to get him into the stalls. That is what he was like – completely genuine in a race but too keen to lark around beforehand.

He jumped off well and settled down as Broadway Flyer made the early pace with Strategic Choice. Environment Friend was in front of me, Winged Love and Carnegie on my inner, Pentire behind. I was not keeping an eye on any other runner in particular – if anything I thought the Arc winner Carnegie more of a danger than Pentire – and my main concern was keeping my colt going easily. So we slotted in behind, went a good pace early on and then eased up a little.

Ascot's short straight means that it is dangerous to try to make up too much ground from the home turn, and unless you have a horse with an explosive turn of foot you have to build up your run coming up the stretch from Swinley Bottom. Lammtarra in the Derby appeared to have a tremendous turn of foot, but in reality that was a combination of the horse finding his stride and the leaders rapidly coming to the end of their tether. At Ascot I couldn't expect him to accelerate instantly, so I had to get him to speed up gradually – to get a little nearer, then a little nearer still. When I asked him to take closer order he at first responded as I'd thought he might, running green and taking a little bit of time to get the message. But get the message he gradually did, and started going forward. I had to niggle him along, but he wasn't losing any ground.

We were approaching the turn when one of the French runners gave Environment Friend a bump, and he in turn nudged us: Lammtarra stumbled, but that seemed to wake him up. Once in the straight I was working hard on him, though I was worried that something with a turn of foot would collar him inside the final furlong. He was running on, running on, and everything else seemed to be coming off the bridle – when all of a sudden here came Michael Hills on Pentire.

SHIT! He came to me on the bridle and apparently coasting, ready to pick us off. People criticised Michael afterwards for coming too soon on Pentire, but what did those critics expect him to do? You've got the Derby winner in front of you, you've got him and everything else covered and your horse is picking up his bit and coming good. Of course you go for home: I and any other jockey would have done the same.

So I was on the inner, pushing Lammtarra for all I was worth, Pentire was outside us and looking as if he had the race at his mercy. But Michael was not going clear, and I thought: once you come off the bridle, I've got you! When Pentire went a neck up I thought he had me cooked, and then I remembered Walter's words: dig deep, and he'll find. I dug deep, gave him a few back-handers, and felt his huge engine working harder and harder. Lammtarra just refused to give in, and as Pentire ran out of petrol forged his way back into the lead to win by a neck.

'Then I remembered Walter's words: "Dig deep, and he'll find."'

It was a thrilling race to win – and probably my best ride. People don't realise how much pressure can be added to a jockey by that sort of background to a race. It's easy to ride a 16–1 shot to whom few give a second thought, but riding the Derby winner in the King George, and after all that fuss over Walter – that's real pressure. I was just delighted that I'd ridden Lammtarra in the way I did: had I ridden him for a turn of foot, he certainly would have been beaten.

His victory in the Arc was wonderful but very different from the King George, as by then everybody knew what this horse was made of. I knew him much better myself – and from the King George was aware, especially, of how deep he would dig in a race. He certainly dug in at Longchamp, showing the heart of a lion to hold off the late challenge of Freedom Cry.

Lammtarra was some horse!

So, of course, was Lochsong, and I shouldn't talk about the race of my life without giving her at least an honourable mention. I won the Prix de l'Abbaye on her twice and plenty of other big races, but the one which stands out is the Palace House Stakes at Newmarket on Two Thousand Guineas Day 1994. I'd been beaten a short head on Grand Lodge in the Classic, but in the very next race Lochsong gave me the most exhilarating ride of my life. Her trainer Ian Balding thought she wasn't fully fit, but she slammed out of the starting gates and I just sat motionless as she found her stride and showed blistering pace all the way to beat Tropical by three lengths and break the course record by almost a second – an astonishing performance. I've never been that fast on a horse – it was just like a surfer hitting a good wave.

Incredible! 99

Walter Swinburn

All Along in the Trusthouse Forte Prix de l'Arc de Triomphe, Longchamp, 2 October 1983

THEY STILL CALL HIM 'THE CHOIRBOY', EVEN though he's now well into his mid-thirties. But if Walter Swinburn's nickname is difficult to dislodge, so is his reputation for being one of the coolest and finest big-race jockeys in the world.

That reputation was earned very young. He won the Derby on Shergar in 1981 at the age of nineteen – the youngest winning rider of that race since eighteen-year-old Lester Piggott in 1954 – and before long had added countless Classics and other big races around the globe.

Walter Swinburn was born in Oxford on 7 August 1961, the son of former leading Irish jockey Wally Swinburn. He was apprenticed to Frenchie Nicholson, father of David Nicholson and fabled nurturer of embryonic talent, riding his first winner on Paddy's Luck at Kempton Park on 12 July 1978. He joined Newmarket trainer Michael Stoute and in 1981 steered the Aga Khan's Shergar to an extraordinary ten-length victory in the Derby. Like many up-and-coming superstar jockeys, Swinburn occasionally fell foul of the stewards in his early riding years, and was serving out a suspension when Shergar went on to win the Irish Derby (Lester Piggott picked up a useful spare ride), though reunited with the colt to win the King George VI and Queen Elizabeth Diamond Stakes at Ascot.

Since then Swinburn's fame as a big-race jockey has been firmly established and consolidated by further success in the English Classics: the One Thousand Guineas with Musical Bliss (1989), Hatoof (1992) and Sayyedati (1993); the Two Thousand Guineas with Doyoun (1988); two more Derbies with Shahrastani (1986) and Lammtarra (1995); and the Oaks with Unite (1987). In addition he has won the Arc on All Along (1983) and countless other big races around the world.

It was this globe-trotting aspect of Swinburn's career which brought him to the headlines in February 1996, when a fall from a two-year-old named Liffey River in a race at Sha Tin in Hong Kong caused multiple injuries and landed him in intensive care. The speed of his recovery is testimony to the toughness and resilience of one of the most skilled and popular Flat jockeys of his era.

" I did not ride Shergar as a two-year-old – Lester partnered him in his two races – but rode him work before his first race at three and found him workmanlike rather than spectacular. But he certainly won in spectacular fashion on his three-year-old debut, by ten lengths in the Guardian Classic Trial at Sandown Park, then took the Chester Vase by twelve lengths and became a red-hot favourite for the Derby.

Shergar gave me a dream ride at Epsom. He jumped out, found his own pace and lobbed along as the leaders went off at a million miles an hour, with me just putting my hands down on his withers and letting him travel at his own speed. Going down the hill I had to switch him out from behind to avoid interference, and he just pulled his way to the front, taking up the running early in the straight and striding home. That horse could gallop!

Shahrastani was a very different sort. The 1986 Derby has gone down as the one which Dancing Brave lost rather than Shahrastani won, but the day Shahrastani won the Irish Derby by eight lengths he was a very good colt indeed: Greville Starkey, who had ridden Dancing Brave at Epsom, flew back from Ireland with us and said that Dancing Brave might well not have beaten Shahrastani in that form.

As for Lammtarra, his Derby win in 1995 gave me an incredible feeling. I'd ridden him in his only race as a two-year-old, at Newbury, where he was flat to the boards until I gave him one little smack. All of a sudden he moved up about two gears and flew, winning from the hot favourite Myself. What happened next was extraordinary. I just couldn't pull him up, eventually having to stand right up in my irons and pull his head round. Once turned round and facing the stands, he then tried to take off again!

His trainer Alex Scott was so keen on the colt that he backed him for the 1995 Derby at 33–1, but less than two months after that Newbury debut Alex was murdered at his stud near Newmarket. I was devastated. I'd ridden a lot for him during his short training career, and for him to be struck down in that way was appalling. It made Lammtarra – for whom Alex had such high hopes – a very special horse for me.

I thought a lot about him during the winter, and in the spring went to see him in Dubai on my way back from Hong Kong. Despite his lung problems he looked well, and I was delighted when Simon Crisford of Godolphin asked me to ride him in the Derby. I galloped him the week before the race, and though he was not a great worker, tending to do just enough, what he did he managed in a very effortless way. There was something very special about him, but in some ways he was a funny horse. He would come out on the gallops and plant – just stand there, refusing to move. You'd have to leave him alone a minute or two until he was ready to get on, and let him have his own way. Nor was he a great respecter of persons: he even did his planting act one morning when Sheikh Mohammed had come to watch him work! It was not that the horse was in any way ungenuine – just his own boss. I liked that about him.

In a race Lammtarra was a bottomless pit: you could keep asking him and he'd find more. Of course, we didn't know this before the Derby, and there was naturally some concern that running him in that race after just one outing as a two-year-old and without a previous run at three would be too much for the horse. Yet he was such a character that if any inexperienced horse could withstand the hurly-burly it was him, and in the event getting squeezed up by another runner after about a furlong and a half actually worked in his favour. It meant that I could rein him back and tuck him in, which was just what I wanted, and from the top of the hill I was travelling, travelling, travelling – and praying: daylight! daylight! daylight! All of a sudden my prayers were answered. They opened up in front of me, I whacked him a couple, got a response, and away we went. Every time I asked Lammtarra something he delivered, and a furlong out I thought I'd be placed. Half a furlong out I thought: he's going to win! – and he swept past the three in front to get up just before the post. I've never had a feeling like that.

I did not ride Lammtarra again, Godolphin choosing to replace me with Frankie for the King George. To this day I don't know why I lost the ride: it hurt, but I had to accept the decision and get on.

My partnership with the great French filly All Along also ended with my losing the ride, but we had some fantastic times together, and despite those three Derby wins, the 1983 Arc on All Along would have to be the race on which, more than any other, I look back with satisfaction.

I only got the Arc ride after Lester Piggott, Greville Starkey, Freddie Head, Gary Moore, Cash Asmussen and Joe Mercer had all, for one reason

'All Along just started devouring the ground' – and she wins the 1983 Arc from Sun Princess and Luth Enchantee (no. 24).

or another, declined. (In Lester's case his decision to ride Awaasif rather than All Along caused a split with All Along's owner Daniel Wildenstein which eventually led to Lester losing the job as stable jockey to Henry Cecil.)

When All Along's trainer Patrick-Louis Biancone called to offer me the ride my initial reaction was simply one of pleasure at getting a mount in Europe's biggest race, since my intended ride, the Irish Derby winner Shareef Dancer, had been retired, and it looked as if the Arc would pass me by that year. But when I went across to France to ride work on All Along I realised that she was not just an Arc ride – she'd be going into the race with a very good chance indeed.

All Along was then a four-year-old. At three she'd won the Prix Vermeille and finished runner-up in the Japan Cup, and though she'd taken some time to find her form at four all the signs were that she was coming right for the Arc, running second to Time Charter in the Prix Foy at Longchamp three weeks before the big race. She'd been trained with the Arc in mind and had not had a hard season, and in her final gallop the week before the race she worked brilliantly, going ten lengths clear of her galloping companions. She was fresh, strong, and ready to run for her life. By the time I was on the plane home from France I was convinced that she was in with a shout.

My first ride in the Arc had also been for Patrick. In 1981 I'd gone across to ride the great sprinting filly Marwell in the Prix de l'Abbaye – she won, beating Sharpo – and, having offered me an Arc ride on the outsider Gap Of Dunloe, he showed me films of previous runnings. Local wisdom is that it's best to go up the inner, and take the chance of not meeting interference, rather than go wide. Never, they say, make your move before the final straight: if you pick your horse up before that final straight you won't get home. This is curious but true: at some British racecourses you can set your horse alight four furlongs out and still get home; at Longchamp, you move before that final short straight at your peril.

It was a typically strong Arc field. The 1982 Oaks winner Time Charter, who earlier in the season had won the King George before beating All Along in the Prix Foy, was favourite, with 1983 Oaks and St Leger winner Sun Princess strongly fancied along with Diamond Shoal, runner-up to Time Charter at Ascot, and the tough Irish mare Stanerra.

All Along was drawn towards the outside, which suited me well enough as I wanted to drop her out. I let her miss the kick and tack over towards the inner, keeping her towards the back of the field as we made our way up the hill. She was travelling really sweetly, and I was able to creep up into a more prominent position without too much effort. At the top of the hill she was tracking horses, and then on the downhill run I set her alight up the inside.

As I asked her to quicken I could see that my way up the inner was blocked by Bruce Raymond on Seymour Hicks, and for one horrible second I thought I might get stopped. But then Bruce picked up his whip in his right hand, Seymour Hicks drifted off the rail, and that was it: we were through. Turning into the straight I knew she had a great chance of being placed, though Sun Princess was making the best of her way home and was clearly

'To kick like she did and kick again was the mark of a very great filly'

23

Trusthouse Forte Prix de l'Arc de Triomphe

Longchamp, 2 October 1983		$1\frac{1}{2}$ miles
1 ALL ALONG	W. R. Swinburn	173–10
2 Sun Princess	W. Carson	27–4
3 Luth Enchantee	M. Philipperon	17–1

Also ran: Time Charter (4th), Salmon Leap, Stanerra, Lovely Dancer, Zalataia, Lancastrian, Marie de Litz, Sagace, Diamond Shoal, Awaasif, Seymour Hicks, Orofino, Prima Voce, General Holme, Guns Of Navarone, Escaline, Dalby Jaguar, Sharaya, Welsh Term, Don Pasquini, Acamas, Dzudo, Sailor's Dance

26 ran	*1 length, short neck*

---

not stopping. Then in the last two hundred metres All Along just started devouring the ground. I switched her away from the rails and she flew past Diamond Shoal, Time Charter, Stanerra, and finally Sun Princess to hit the front close home and win, going away, by a length. Sun Princess was second and Luth Enchantee came with a wet sail to finish third.

It had been a mind-boggling turn of foot, an unbelievable run, and everything in the race had gone just right. We had a wonderful reception as we came back past the stands, with the crowd going mad, people spilling out on to the track – just bedlam. They were ecstatic at having a French-trained winner.

Lester, who'd got off All Along to ride the unplaced Awaasif, congratulated me afterwards, but I'd love to know how he felt six weeks later after All Along had gone to North America and landed the treble of the Rothmans International at Woodbine in Toronto, the Turf Classic at Aqueduct in New York, and the Washington DC International at Laurel Park – a combination which brought connections a million-dollar bonus in addition to huge prize money. I think missing the jockey's percentage of that lot must really have hurt Lester!

All Along adapted brilliantly to the different tracks, and showed herself to be an amazingly tough filly. Just two weeks after the Arc she beat Thunder Puddles in the Rothmans, a week later cruised round Aqueduct to beat the same horse eight lengths in the Turf Classic despite my dropping my whip, and three weeks after that beat Welsh Term in the International – where for the first time that autumn she gave me the feeling of being tired. She won well, but the exertions were just beginning to take their toll.

All Along ran in the Arc again as a five-year-old, having had the rather unorthodox preparation of an outing in the Turf Classic at Belmont Park, New York. She had a dream run again but that year the kick was missing, and she could only run on to finish third behind her stable companion

Sagace. Then she was off on her travels again, aiming for a repeat win in the Rothmans International at Woodbine. That's where I got sacked, as Patrick thought I had not ridden her to instructions. The fact was that she was no longer the superb racehorse she'd been in 1983, but I was out on my ear, and that was that. Angel Cordero rode her in the Breeders' Cup Turf at Hollywood Park, where she was beaten a neck by Lashkari; she did not race again.

It's always difficult to compare horses. Zilzal was probably the most electrifying horse I ever rode. Sonic Lady, Marwell, Shadeed and Hatoof were all marvellous. Shergar was a relentless galloper and Lammtarra had such heart. But I'd have to put All Along up there with the best, and on Arc day 1983 she was absolutely brilliant. To kick like she did and then kick again was the mark of a very great filly. **99**

John Francome

Sea Pigeon in the Waterford Crystal Champion Hurdle, Cheltenham, 17 March 1981

JOHN MCCRIRICK CALLS HIS CHANNEL Four Racing colleague John Francome 'Greatest Jockey', and it's not hard to see why.

The rider of 1,138 winners over jumps in a fifteen-year career which ended in 1985, Francome established for himself a reputation as one of the sport's supreme stylists, unmatched among his generation of jump jockeys at putting his horse at a fence, and a brilliant all-round horseman.

Son of a Swindon builder, John Francome was born on 13 December 1952, and had already made a big name for himself as a junior show jumper – he won international honours at the sport – before in 1969 joining the Lambourn yard of trainer Fred Winter, with whom he remained for his entire riding career. On his first ride in public, at Worcester on 2 December 1970, he won a three-mile hurdle on a horse named Multigrey. On his second ride in public he fell and broke his wrist.

In 1975 Francome became Winter's stable jockey on the retirement of Richard Pitman, and ended the 1975–6 season champion jockey for the first time. In all he won the championship seven times, including the 1981–2 season when he shared the title with Peter Scudamore: Scu had built up a big lead before being sidelined through injury, and once Francome had caught up with his rival he stopped riding for the last few days of the season in order that the title should be tied, a sporting gesture emblematic of the camaraderie among National Hunt jockeys.

John Francome never won the Grand National – second on Rough And Tumble in 1980 was the closest he came – but he did land the Cheltenham Gold Cup in 1978 for Fred Winter on Midnight Court and the Champion Hurdle in 1981 on Sea Pigeon, trained by Peter Easterby. Other famous horses with whom he was associated included Bula, Burrough Hill Lad, Brown Chamberlin, Wayward Lad and Lanzarote.

He retired from the saddle towards the end of the 1984–5 season, his decision to quit hastened by a fall at Chepstow. As he wrote in his autobiography *Born Lucky*: 'I parted company with The Reject at the open ditch and as he did so he galloped all over me. I am not superstitious as a rule but I took this as a hint that it was time to pack up and so that's what I did.'

After a brief spell as a trainer John Francome turned his attention to writing and broadcasting for Channel Four Racing, where his experience in the saddle gave him a special insight into the sport he had so graced during his riding years.

His approach to the task of choosing the race of his life is characteristically frank:

66 If I'm totally honest, there are very few races from my riding career that I can remember in much detail! I never watch videos of the races I rode, and don't go over the top about the horses: I once described them as the tools of my trade and would not go back on that, though obviously some races were special. The 1978 Gold Cup on Midnight Court, for example, meant a very great deal to me as it was Fred Winter's first win in the race. He'd been trying for so long, had had so many of his runners start favourite, and had experienced such bad luck in the race, that it was wonderful to be able to win it for him at last. He'd been very loyal to me when I was having difficulties with the Jockey Club over my supposed links with the bookmaker John Banks: Fred could easily have thrown me out – and plenty of other trainers would have done so – but he stuck by me.

I suppose the 1981 Champion Hurdle on Sea Pigeon must be the race of my life – not because I had to ride particularly brilliantly to win it, but because Sea Pigeon was such a great horse.

He wasn't really my ride at all. I was standing in for his usual rider Jonjo O'Neill, who had broken his leg at Bangor in October 1980. It was clear that Jonjo would be very hard pressed to get back in time for Cheltenham, and Sea Pigeon's trainer Peter Easterby phoned and asked if I wanted to ride the horse. I said I would.

By this time Sea Pigeon had already won one Champion Hurdle – as well as countless other races, including the Ebor Handicap on the Flat – so I knew plenty about him, including that he was a funny old horse with loads of ability but the inclination to pull himself up once he got to the front. The first

---

Waterford Crystal Champion Hurdle

Cheltenham, 17 March 1981   *2 miles*

1 SEA PIGEON	J. Francome	7–4 fav
2 Pollardstown	P. Blacker	9–1
3 Daring Run	Mr T. Walsh	8–1

Also ran: Starfen (4th), Slaney Idol, Celtic Ryde, Bird's Nest, Going Strait, Heighlin, Badsworth Boy, Martie's Anger, Meladon, Mount Harvard, Ivan King

14 ran $1\frac{1}{2}$ *lengths, neck*

time I ever sat on him was when I got the leg-up in the paddock before the Holsten Diat Pils Hurdle at Sandown Park in November 1980. He hadn't run for a while and the lass who led him up told me he might be a bit short of a race, so I was not expecting too many fireworks, but Sandown with its uphill finish has always been a good place to get the feel of Cheltenham prospects, and this was the ideal introduction to him. I didn't put him into the race until jumping the last and still thought he was going to pull up, but he ran on well to the line to beat Celtic Ryde half a length.

'He was a joy to ride'

I didn't ride him when he won his next race, the Fighting Fifth Hurdle at Newcastle, and when I walked into the parade ring before the Champion Hurdle I asked Peter Easterby how the horse was. Peter told me he was ten pounds better than he'd been last year. Since in 1980 he'd beaten Monksfield by seven lengths this sounded good enough to me, and that was all Peter said, apart from a parting shot of 'I'll leave him to you.'

Although he was now eleven years old, it was clear to me that Sea Pigeon would win that Champion Hurdle so long as he got a clear round: he was simply in a different class from everything else in the race. I remember tracking the outsider Ivan King on the run to the first hurdle, thinking will I go to the left of him or the right of him? You should never get close in behind one horse, but I was lucky: Ivan King fell and rolled one way as I went the other way. Pure luck, but had it gone otherwise I'd never have won.

The trick with Sea Pigeon was simply not to hit the front too soon, or he'd put his head in the air and think he'd done enough. At the top of the hill I had to take a pull, so well was he going, and I kept restraining him so that at the last we were third behind Daring Run and Pollardstown, with Starfen just behind us. With most horses there would have been the worry of having to make up ground if you hit the last, but Sea Pigeon had so much in hand that day it wouldn't have mattered, and I can't think of many horses who could have been travelling as easily in a Champion Hurdle. I waited until halfway up the run-in before putting him into the lead, but I could easily have waited another fifty yards and still have won. Once I eased him past the two in front he ran to the line and won by a length and a half from Pollardstown.

People said it was an amazingly cool performance, but as far as I was concerned it was nothing of the kind. You know how you're going, and winning the Champion Hurdle like that was no more difficult than being instructed to have your horse join in halfway up a gallop.

Unlike most old hurdlers, who just keep galloping, Sea Pigeon had loads of speed and real class. He was a joy to ride.

My other lasting riding memory is also of a hurdler – one with a mind of his own: Derring Rose, who in the very next race after Sea Pigeon's Champion Hurdle in 1981 bolted up in the Stayers' Hurdle. That horse was

John Francome and Sea Pigeon (left) bide their time as Pollardstown (blinkers) and Daring Run lead over the last.

29

a law unto himself, a real old character who used to walk backwards to the gallops with his ears pricked. My brother-in-law took him hunting once, and Derring Rose ran backwards and fell into a canal: they had to swim him down about half a mile before they could get him out where the sides weren't sheer.

In the Colt Car Corinium Hurdle at Cheltenham on New Year's Eve 1981 he dug in his heels on the way to the start, so I had to get off and lug him down to the starting area. He then tried as usual to pull himself up as we were going down the hill on the stretch away from the stands. I managed to keep him going and he caught hold of the bridle again, making up an amazing amount of ground to catch the leader Heighlin. Halfway up the run-in the mulish side of Derring Rose threatened to get the better of him, but without resorting to the whip – which would have been fatal – I managed to coax him home, and he won by three lengths. It looked like a ride of great determination and all that, but the real reason I didn't want him to stop where he first decided he might, on that downhill stretch, was that it would have taken me a bloody long time to get back to the weighing-room from there.

I loved Derring Rose: he was the closest you'd ever get to having a horse talk to you, and more than any horse I ever rode, he knew what was what. **99**

Adrian Maguire

Viking Flagship in the Mumm Melling Chase, Aintree, 7 April 1995

THE INFANT PHENOMENON. To encapsulate the impact of Adrian Maguire since he exploded on to the National Hunt scene in Britain in 1991, you could do worse than filch the accolade Charles Dickens bestowed on the young actress Miss Ninetta Crummles in *Nicholas Nickleby*.

For what else was Maguire but another Infant Phenomenon? One of ten children of a green-keeper in Kilmessan, County Meath, he was born on 29 April 1971. Having cut his riding teeth on the pony-racing circuits of his native Ireland, where he rode his first winner (weighing in at five stone seven pounds) at the age of twelve, he graduated to the point-to-point field. By the time he won the Irish point-to-point riders' championship in the 1990–1 season he had already got off the mark under Rules – on Gladtogetit in a bumper at Sligo on 11 February 1990 – and made his mark in the top flight of jumping on both sides of the Irish Sea.

If the name 'Mr A. Maguire' against Martin Pipe's runner Omerta in the Fulke Walwyn Kim Muir Chase on the opening day of the 1991 Cheltenham Festival meant little to the great majority of racegoers before the race, it counted for a great deal afterwards. Maguire, who had never before been to Cheltenham, let alone ridden there, showed the skills of a jockey far senior to his nineteen years to bring the gelding home a twelve-length winner. The following month he announced himself a major new talent when getting the same horse home by a short head from Cahervillahow in a rousing finish to the Irish Grand National, and a star was born.

A remote third in that Irish National was Cool Ground, trained by Toby Balding, and when Maguire moved to England for the 1991–2 season he teamed up with Balding to form a highly successful partnership which culminated in Cool Ground's short-head victory over The Fellow in the 1992 Cheltenham Gold Cup. That season Maguire came eighth in the jockeys' championship. In 1992–3 he finished third behind Richard Dunwoody and Peter Scudamore, and in 1993–4 came just four winners short of Dunwoody's total after the closest contest of recent years. Maguire's tally of 194 was the highest ever recorded by a rider who did not win the title, and included a brilliant victory in the King George VI Chase at Kempton Park on Barton Bank, trained by David Nicholson, for whom Maguire was by then retained jockey.

Maguire's role as heir apparent to Richard Dunwoody has been undermined in subsequent seasons by a string of interruptions as a result of injury, but it would be a reckless punter who bet against his being champion before long. A far safer bet would be on the shortlist of the races of his riding life so far.

" It has to be between the 1993 King George on Barton Bank, which gave me more all-round satisfaction than any race I've won, and the 1995 Mumm Melling Chase on Viking Flagship, the most exciting finish I've ever ridden in.

Winning the Gold Cup on Cool Ground was of course a great thrill, but I think that, being only twenty, I perhaps didn't appreciate it enough at the time. Cool Ground wasn't very quick, but he was a good jumper and would gallop for ever. His owner Peter Bolton invited me down to Whitcombe and asked me to ride at Cheltenham: I was delighted to accept, though I could not quite share his conviction that the horse had a genuine chance of winning the Gold Cup: like many people I felt that Carvill's Hill

'All three flew it and landed running': left to right, Martha's Son, Viking Flagship and Deep Sensation.

was unbeatable in that Gold Cup as long as he jumped round. After all, when Carvill's Hill won the Welsh National at Chepstow in 1991, Cool Ground had pulled up behind him, exhausted like everything else that ran against Carvill's Hill that day.

In the paddock before the Gold Cup, Toby Balding suggested I keep an eye on The Fellow and never be too far away from him: take your time, slowly creep into the race. So in the early stages I kept near the French horse, towards the back, and though I saw Carvill's Hill blunder at the first I was not going to be distracted by what was going on at the head of the field. Halfway round the second circuit Adam Kondrat moved The Fellow up and I went with him, then at the top of the hill I saw that Scu was niggling along on Carvill's Hill. I was going much better than him, and realised that I was in with a real shout. Turning into the straight with two fences to jump there were three of us still with a chance: Cool Ground, The Fellow and Docklands Express. I got the inside rail, but after the second last The Fellow sprinted clear and it looked all over. But I kept going at my horse, and he responded so well that we were upsides The Fellow at the last, with Docklands Express right there with us. I still had the inner and I knew that Cool Ground's stamina would come into play up the hill, so I kept after him and we got up to win by a short head.

I knew I'd been pretty hard on the horse and was punished for it later, but my explanation to the stewards was simple: I hadn't abused him, he responded to every stroke of the whip, and if I hadn't been that hard I wouldn't have won. Toby Balding supported this view, telling the stewards that Cool Ground would not have won had I missed him once. The stewards doubtless knew this as well, but rules are rules, and I was suspended for four days.

The King George on Barton Bank also had a sting in the tail, as both I and Declan Murphy, rider of the runner-up Bradbury Star, were given two-day suspensions for hitting our horses 'with unreasonable frequency' in a desperately close finish. Declan appealed and had his suspension withdrawn, but as far as I was concerned I'd broken the rule, and that was that.

Barton Bank had much more class than Cool Ground, but his problem in his early years over fences was his jumping. At home he would jump brilliantly, but once he got on to a racecourse he would get very keyed up. He was very strong and keen, and if horses were taking him on he'd always want to get his head in front of them, so that often he was doing too much by the time he came to a fence, going too fast and not thinking about how to get over the obstacle; and he tended not to round his back when jumping. He could hit one hard and take the next in his stride. You just never knew exactly what he was going to do, and had to try to tell him everything.

But he could be brilliant, and that King George was his greatest moment. He'd beaten Cab On Target in a two-runner race at Sandown Park before going to Kempton, and we were very hopeful of a good run, though he faced some pretty good opponents, including The Fellow, Young Hustler, Bradbury Star and Travado. Before the race David Nicholson – for whom I was then in my first season as stable jockey – said: go out and enjoy yourself; if he wants to bowl along, let him, but make sure there's enough in the tank to get home.

Mumm Melling Chase

Aintree, 7 April 1995   2½ *miles*

1	VIKING FLAGSHIP	A. Maguire	5–2
2	Deep Sensation	N. Williamson	5–1
3	Martha's Son	R. Farrant	11–10 fav

Also ran: Southolt (4th), Nakir, Second Schedual

6 ran   *short head, 1 length*

Martin Pipe's Rolling Ball, who usually made the running, jumped off in front with Young Hustler, then took it up. I was upsides him for much of the first circuit, and kept outjumping him – so much so that coming past the stands first time round I took up the running. At the last down the far side Barton Bank got it wrong and hit the fence hard, so I sat quiet and got a blow into him on the turn into the home straight before kicking on after the third last. He responded wonderfully, but just after the second last I could see Declan on Bradbury Star looming up on the stands side. All I was concentrating on then was a good jump at the last, as the Kempton run-in is very short and there would be little time to recover from a mistake. Barton Bank flew it and we went for the line, with Bradbury Star coming at us all the time, but my lad just put his head down and wouldn't let the other horse past. We won by a head, and just beyond the finishing line Barton Bank showed what he thought of Bradbury Star's challenge by baring his teeth and trying to bite him!

To win a major race like the King George on Barton Bank – not the easiest of rides – was very special, not least because it was my first big winner for David Nicholson, and my hundredth of that season.

The following year's King George on Barton Bank was very different. Going to the last we were well clear, and winning much easier than in 1993. We were meeting the fence on a long stride: I asked him up, he put down, hit the fence halfway up and shot me out of the saddle. If the 1993 King George was the highest moment of my career to date, the 1994 running was certainly the lowest.

A far happier occasion, and my greatest race to look back on, was the ride on Viking Flagship in the 1995 Mumm Melling Chase at Aintree.

I first rode Viking Flagship in a chase at Haydock Park in December 1993. He was beaten by the only other runner, Last 'O' The Bunch, and I have to admit that at the time he did not excite me at all – a nice handy sort of horse, not over-big and a good jumper, but that was all, and not even, as far as I was concerned, the best two-mile chaser in David Nicholson's yard. When he ran in the Victor Chandler Chase at Warwick in January 1994 I opted to ride the stable's other runner, Waterloo Boy. Richard Dunwoody rode Viking Flagship and duly won, after which I was not going to make the same mistake again, and the horse just kept on getting better and better.

He gave me one of my greatest moments in the Queen Mother Champion Chase at the 1994 Cheltenham Festival. Deep Sensation and Travado were just up on me going to the last: I asked Viking Flagship for a long one, he took it brilliantly, and we outbattled them up the hill.

He repeated his win in the Queen Mother in 1995 – at the meeting I missed, following the sudden death of my mother – and was then aimed at the Mumm Melling Chase at Aintree. The doubt here was whether he would truly stay the trip of two and a half miles – he had not won a chase over that trip – and an additional factor was that the ground was a little bit on the quick side for him. The opposition was top-notch, headed by Tim Forster's brilliant Martha's Son, who had gone through the season unbeaten in five races and had missed Cheltenham in order to be spot-on for the Aintree race, and Deep Sensation.

We were in the front rank all the way round, and as we turned into the straight behind the leader Southolt I took a quick look to see where Deep Sensation was, then a glance to the other side to find Martha's Son, who had not been jumping at his best but was still looking very dangerous. I just kept squeezing along, getting closer and closer to Southolt and gradually getting upsides. At the second last Rodney Farrant and Martha's Son came alongside me and going to the last they appeared to be going the better; then Norman Williamson on Deep Sensation arrived on the inside, and as Southolt faded the three of us, in a line, went hammer and tongs for the fence.

Had one of us missed the last his chance would have gone, but all three flew it and landed running. The other two seemed to pick up slightly better than Viking Flagship, and for a stride or two I thought we were not going to get there. Martha's Son faltered and Deep Sensation took a narrow lead, but halfway up the short run-in my fellow started galloping on again. He just didn't know how to give in, and launched into one final effort to catch Deep Sensation right on the line.

I thought I'd won by a good head – and Norman Williamson agreed – but when Viking Flagship's lad came to lead the horse in he said it was so close no one knew. Certainly David Nicholson was not confident. I started to get worried, and unsaddled outside the winner's enclosure rather than tempt fate and go in. When the verdict came it was a great relief: Viking Flagship by a short head.

I've looked many times at the video of that race. If you slow down the picture as they past the post, you can see that Deep Sensation is lengthening more than Viking Flagship: my horse's head is coming up, Deep Sensation's is going down. Half a stride later Viking Flagship is nearly a neck in front.

That was the most thrilling race I've ever taken part in, but when you go out to ride you don't think of any race as special. Of course it's good to look back on the big moments, to remember what turned out to be a great race, but beforehand you don't care what the race is. You just give your best. 99

'Beforehand you don't care what the race is. You just give your best'

Graham McCourt

Rodeo Star in the Tote Gold Trophy, Newbury, 8 February 1992

WHEN GRAHAM MCCOURT RETURNED to the unsaddling enclosure at Chepstow after winning the Pardubice Handicap Chase on Sister Stephanie on 27 March 1996, he was coming to the end of a riding career which had made him the sixth most successful National Hunt jockey of all. Sister Stephanie was his 921st victory in Britain, a total which left him just two short of that accumulated by the legendary Fred Winter, with only Peter Scudamore, Richard Dunwoody, John Francome and Stan Mellor having crossed into the magic land of four figures. McCourt's 921 is the highest career total for a jump jockey who was never champion.

Careful readers of the form book will have noted that as one career was ending another was in its early stages – for Sister Stephanie was not just ridden but trained by Graham McCourt, who had taken out a trainer's licence earlier in the year.

McCourt's farewell to the saddle brought with it much appreciation for a notable riding life which had spanned twenty-one years: the *Sporting Life*, for example, described it as 'hallmarked by uncompromising professionalism'.

Graham McCourt was born – on 17 August 1959 – into a racing family: his father Matthew had been a professional jump jockey for many years, and after retiring from the saddle became a trainer in Letcombe Regis, near Wantage. McCourt junior was apprenticed to his father and to David Nicholson, and rode his first winner at the age of sixteen on Vulrory's Kid in an amateur riders' Flat race at Ascot on 27 September 1975. (To apply some historical perspective: this was the same card on which Rose Bowl won her first Queen Elizabeth II Stakes, with Two Thousand Guineas winner Bolkonski back in fourth.) His first win over jumps was registered when Playful Warrior won an amateur riders' hurdle at Wolverhampton on Boxing Day the same year.

Although Graham McCourt was never champion jockey, he achieved one feat on which plenty of champions have missed out: winning the two biggest races of the Cheltenham National Hunt Festival. In 1990 he won a sensational Gold Cup on Norton's Coin, at 100–1 the longest-priced winner ever of the most important steeplechase in the calendar; two years later he added the Champion Hurdle on the novice Royal Gait. Among dozens of other big-race victories was the 1988 Breeders' Cup Steeplechase at Fair Hill on Jimmy Lorenzo.

For the race of his life, however, we stay closer to home, at Newbury.

66 They say that what matters is the taking part, but that's wrong. It's the winning that matters!

Norton's Coin and Royal Gait each gave me very special moments in my riding career. Royal Gait was trained by James Fanshawe, a wonderful trainer whom I'd known for a long time, and Norton's Coin was of course a fairy tale. Before the race I thought he was probably good enough to finish third or fourth, and had he been trained by Jenny Pitman or Jimmy FitzGerald rather than some daft old dairy farmer named Sirrell Griffiths he'd never have started at 100–1. I still have a laugh with Sirrell about it whenever I see him.

But, to be blunt, both Norton's Coin and Royal Gait were horses which I just happened to ride, and the race which gave me the greatest overall satisfaction was the 1992 Tote Gold Trophy on Rodeo Star. He was trained by Nigel Tinkler, whom I had known very well for years – one of his owners had a horse with my father – and who had become a great friend. I was with Nigel at the sales when he bought Rodeo Star, and I used to ride the horse out. I schooled him the first time over hurdles, and got to know him closely. He was a lovely horse – a very easy-going character, happy as a sandboy in the yard, just very easy to have around.

Riding Rodeo Star brought me a great deal of pleasure, but his win in the Royal Garden Hotel Hurdle at Kempton Park on Boxing Day 1991 was especially satisfying: his owners had a fair few quid on and he didn't let them down. For most of the race we vied for the lead with Warren Marston and a nice four-year-old hurdler of David Nicholson's called Viking Flagship, and Warren and I did a great deal of talking trying to settle into a pace which would suit us both. Viking Flagship dropped away in the straight but Rodeo Star kept on well to beat Monday Club a length.

Rodeo Star met Viking Flagship again in a handicap hurdle at Ascot in January 1992 and, ridden by Jamie Osborne, once more beat him easily; and then it was all systems go for the Tote Gold Trophy.

I've always had a soft spot for this race. In the old days when it was still the Schweppes Gold Trophy and I was a claimer I would always look forward to riding in it: it was such a competitive race, sometimes fearsomely so.

Six years old at the time of the Tote Gold Trophy, Rodeo Star had won four races on the trot and was going up in the weights. After a successful career as a juvenile he had lost his way a little and dropped down the handicap, but each time he won during the 1991–2 season he went up a few pounds, and carried ten stone ten in the Newbury race. He was genuine but a little idle, and always quite hard work to ride – not the sort to win by ten lengths easing down, more like two lengths, pushed out.

The Tote Gold Trophy is often the sort of race for a horse at the lower end of the handicap who because of a setback or something else drops down the weights and then miraculously finds ten pounds' improvement. But Rodeo Star went there completely fair and square – on his right handicap mark, fully exposed and in great form. He was fourth favourite that day, with Jimmy FitzGerald's Native Mission joint favourite with Kibreet and Viking Flagship also preferred in the betting. Bracketed with Rodeo Star on 15–2 at the off was Jenny Pitman's useful six-year-old Egypt Mill Prince, like Viking Flagship soon to make a considerable name for himself over fences. Of the market rivals it was Native Mission I feared most, but I was very hopeful of a big run from my fellow.

I knew that the pace was going to be very fast – it always is in that race – but expected them to go like greased lightning early on and then ease off about halfway round. Sure enough, the leaders went off hell for leather, but I was not going to be panicked on Rodeo Star and kept him tucked in, far enough behind not to go mad but close enough to keep the pressure on. Coming out of the back straight towards the cross flight of hurdles – four out – I shook him up, and from about fifth or sixth position we moved up

Graham McCourt and Rodeo Star (left) head Egypt Mill Prince (right) and Native Mission at the last.

into the lead. He was quite happy running like this, and once he got into top gear was likely to stay there.

I chased him up going into the straight, aware that it was now up to the others to catch me if they could. We raced wide because I wanted to run down the stands rail, where I thought the ground would be best, and knew that they were queuing up behind to come and reel me in. But the harder I worked on the old devil the more he responded. Egypt Mill Prince was travelling very well for Mark Pitman, and Native Mission and Mark Dwyer were mounting a challenge, but still Rodeo Star kept going. He was flat to the boards – but there's flat to the boards and flat to the boards! I was flat out but had still not fully committed him, as with a horse like that you can feel flat out but still keep a bit up your sleeve. He was such a battler: give him a smack and his head goes out another half inch, his stride lengthens that crucial bit and he digs in.

I knew that Mark Dwyer would be holding up Native Mission for a late run. He was the one I wanted to shake off most – and going to the last, out of the corner of my eye I saw them. 'We're in trouble now,' I thought, but

'What counts is winning!'

I also thought – possibly uncharitably – that Native Mission was not the most genuine horse in training and might be worried out of it by a true battler like Rodeo Star. So there was a glimmer of hope.

Coming to the last Native Mission and Egypt Mill Prince were almost upsides, and I knew that the final jump would be crucial. I asked him for a big one and he responded magnificently, jumping it as if it were the first, and then I knew there was a bit more in the tank. When I was still in front eight or nine strides after the last I knew that Native Mission would not be able to get past me, and Rodeo Star kept up his gallop all the way to the line. In the end he won quite easily – five lengths clear at the post, with Egypt Mill Prince half that distance further back in third.

The race took quite a bit out of Rodeo Star, and he didn't win again that season. But in 1993 he won two of the top staying handicaps on the Flat – the Queen's Prize and the Chester Cup – and later went chasing.

The great thing about winning that Tote Gold Trophy on the horse was

Tote Gold Trophy

Newbury, 8 February 1992   *2 miles 100 yards*

1 RODEO STAR	G. McCourt	15–2
2 Native Mission	M. Dwyer	13–2 jt fav
3 Egypt Mill Prince	M. Pitman	15–2

Also ran: Bookcase (4th), Boarding School, Marlingford, Jungle Knife,
One For The Pot, Old Virginia, Viking Flagship, Kibreet, Shannon Glen, Imperial Brush,
Galway Star, Spanish Servant

15 ran   *5 lengths, 2½ lengths*

that we'd planned it all, without hiding the horse's ability in any way, and had all the angles covered. It was a very professional operation, a job well done. But there was also a strong personal element. The trainer was a great friend; I knew the owners well; Newbury is my local track, and I'd always wanted to win that race. Rodeo Star was the perfect partner.

Winning the Champion Hurdle and the Gold Cup were great thrills, but with all the press men waiting outside the shower, on both occasions it felt like there was no time to enjoy the sensation. After Rodeo Star had won at Newbury, on the other hand, I had time to sit back and enjoy it: Nigel and I went for a few drinks afterwards and a real celebration with the owners.

Taking part is OK, but what counts is winning! **"**

Frankie Dettori and Barathea win the 1994 Breeders' Cup Mile at Churchill Downs.

Above: **Just So (Simon Burrough, left) and Miinnehoma (Richard Dunwoody)
at Valentine's Brook second time around in the 1994 Grand National.**
Below: **Dawn Run (Jonjo O'Neill) puts her best feet forward early in the 1986 Cheltenham Gold Cup.**

Willie Carson and Erhaab (extreme left) storm home in the 1994 Derby from King's Theatre (Mick Kinane, white cap) and Colonel Collins (John Reid, spotted cap).

Above: 'A dream ride' for nineteen-year-old Walter Swinburn on Shergar in the 1981 Derby.
Below: John Reid and Tony Bin hold off Michael Roberts and Mtoto in the 1988 Prix de l'Arc de Triomphe.

The camaraderie of jump jockeys: Norman Williamson on the winner Master Oats (left) and
Richard Dunwoody on third-placed Miinnehoma after the 1995 Cheltenham Gold Cup.

Peter Scudamore and Granville Again after the 1993 Champion Hurdle.

Jason Weaver and Mister Baileys before the 1994 Two Thousand Guineas.

Lester Piggott, October 1992.

Kevin Darley and Celtic Swing, 1995.

Willie Carson

Erhaab in the Ever Ready Derby, Epsom, 1 June 1994

WILLIAM FISHER HUNTER CARSON OBE was born in Stirling, Scotland, on 16 November 1942, and over fifty years later was still winning Classic races. He was fifty-one years old when landing the 1994 Derby on Erhaab, only the second rider since the war to win the race at over fifty: Charlie Smirke was also fifty-one when winning on Hard Ridden in 1958.

The first of Carson's haul of winners – 3,776 in Britain at the start of the 1996 season, which puts him third in the list of winning-most jockeys behind Gordon Richards and Lester Piggott – came in an apprentice race at Catterick on 19 July 1962 on a horse named Pinkers Pond. He has been champion jockey on five occasions – 1972, 1973, 1978, 1980 and 1983 – yet notched up his highest total for a domestic season in a year he did not win the title: 187 in 1990, when the championship went to Pat Eddery with 209.

In any analysis of the Carson magic, statistics are far outweighed by other factors: his effervescent personality, his head-down-and-pump-pump-pump riding style and, above all, the sheer quality of the horses he has ridden.

Troy in 1979 provided his first Derby winner, Henbit the following year his second, and Nashwan in 1989 his third. On both Troy and Nashwan he won the King George VI and Queen Elizabeth Diamond Stakes at Ascot, a race he also took on Ela Mana Mou (1980) and Petoski (1985). Then there was the Queen's great filly Dunfermline, winner of the Oaks in 1977, Jubilee year, and later that season the only horse ever to defeat Alleged when winning a famous race for the St Leger. Other great fillies whom Carson has pushed to Classic victory include Salsabil (who in 1990 won the One Thousand Guineas and Oaks before becoming the first filly since 1900 to land the Irish Derby) and 1983 Oaks and St Leger winner Sun Princess.

By the time the 1996 Derby had been run, Carson had won seventeen English Classics – among them the 1988 St Leger on Minster Son, a colt he bred himself – in addition to countless other big races at home and abroad. And yet the horse he rates the greatest he ever rode is no Classic winner but Dayjur, the phenomenally fast sprinter who in 1990 carried all before him in Europe before leaving an unenviable memory as one of the unluckiest losers ever: in the Breeders' Cup Sprint at Belmont Park, New York, he jumped a shadow with the race in his grasp, completely lost his rhythm and was narrowly beaten. 'It was a pleasure to get out of bed in the morning to ride this horse,' Carson wrote in his autobiography: 'When you'd finished, you were tingling.'

But it was the Derby Day crowd who were tingling after his virtuoso performance on Erhaab, owned by Carson's retainer Sheikh Hamdan Al-Maktoum and trained by John Dunlop, in the 1994 Ever Ready Derby.

❝ The first time I rode Erhaab was in a two-year-old maiden race at Newmarket at the end of July 1993. The field included such horses as King's Theatre and Nicolotte – both, like Erhaab, making their debuts. Erhaab was a bit backward and I wasn't going to give him a hard race, so I just went through the motions and let him finish down the field. I was encouraged by the way he kept on in the final quarter of a mile.

Next time out was another maiden, the Yattendon Stakes at Newbury. There were twenty-three runners, with a horse of Peter Chapple-Hyam's named Pencader odds-on favourite: he won easily from Hawajiss, with Erhaab back in twelfth. Again, there was no point in being hard on him as he was still undeveloped.

I didn't ride him in his next race, when he went up to Newcastle and, with Billy Newnes on board, absolutely murdered some good horses. I then rode him in September at Leicester, where he started favourite. Halfway through the race he seemed to have given up, so I picked up my stick, gave him a couple of whacks and he ended up winning by seven lengths. This performance made me realise that he was a far from straightforward horse, a little bit suspect in his mind, and next time out he was beaten a short head when odds-on in a three-horse race at Salisbury.

First time out as a three-year-old he ran in the Feilden Stakes at Newmarket, where he was beaten by Henry Cecil's Cicerao. I rode a normal sort of race, taking my time, and was making my run up the inside when Mick Kinane's horse Daronne rolled towards the rail and I had to snatch up. I got Erhaab balanced, switched him to the outside and then gave him a flick with the whip – and he absolutely flew, being beaten only a neck. Everyone who saw the race knew that Erhaab should have won, and that run convinced me that he needed a longer trip, so I announced on returning to unsaddle: 'This could be a Derby horse.' The remark was half tongue-in-cheek: I thought it possible, but wasn't confident.

Next stop was York for the Dante Stakes, where Erhaab did everything I was hoping he would. Again I found him playing around a bit, so gave him a couple of sharp cracks with the whip and off he went and did it, winning by three and a half lengths from Weigh Anchor, with Two Thousand Guineas winner Mister Baileys third.

After the Dante the situation seemed clear enough to me. We had a horse who should win the Derby on form, but he was not a straightforward ride. He was reluctant to show his true potential and there was some reason why.

Another problem was that he was very slow to warm up: he couldn't go the pace early on and didn't always want to quicken when you asked him, and in the Derby this was a big drawback. For that race, above all others, you need a horse with instant acceleration: when a gap appears you have to go for it. Erhaab, on the other hand, needed to be teed up, got balanced and running before you could really get stuck into him. Epsom is far from the ideal racecourse for a horse like that, which left me in the strange position of knowing that I would be on the best horse on the wrong course!

John Dunlop rarely has his jockeys ride on his home gallops so I did not work Erhaab between the Dante and Epsom, but I did suggest that we might have a problem with him as he was a quirky horse. The Derby is almost always run at a true gallop, and I was planning to take up a good position in the early stages and just sit comfortably, give him plenty of time, and try to keep him out of the hustle and bustle, which I knew he would hate.

Looking at the other runners, there was clearly going to be plenty of pace. Mister Baileys was a confirmed front-runner, as was Broadway Flyer, unbeaten as a three-year-old. John Gosden's Linney Head had won the

Willie Carson and Erhaab (left) swoop past (left to right) Colonel Collins, Mister Baileys and King's Theatre.

Classic Trial at Sandown and was a very live candidate, and the one I was most frightened of was Colonel Collins, trained by Peter Chapple-Hyam. But he was a rather straight-legged horse, which suggested he would not be suited to the undulations of Epsom, and that increased my view that Erhaab could beat him. With Broadway Flyer and Mister Baileys in the field there would be a very fierce pace, but I told myself not to panic if I got too far behind as I knew they'd come back to me in the straight.

There were twenty-five runners, and several seemed to have little chance, taking part in the race purely because it was the Derby. This is a recipe for trouble in running, and the scrimmaging which so often takes place is one of the reasons why many horses who run in it come back lame, sore or with muscle problems. Some never recover mentally from what is always the hardest race of their lives to date, and their nerve goes.

As for the race . . .

. . . Erhaab jumps out of the stalls well enough, then as we make the right-handed bend soon after the start the scrimmaging begins around him. I think I should go forward to get him out of trouble, but my better judgement is telling me not to do it – try to save your horse. I sit still and instead of trying to get in front of a horse I get in behind him. As we cross back to the inner rail I'm about three-quarters of the way down the field, and a worried man. I'm saying to myself: you haven't been in any trouble and yet you're too far back. By the mile pole I'm screaming to myself: YOU'RE IN TROUBLE, YOU'RE TOO FAR BACK! But at least we're motoring and I'm sitting still, and as usual there's a lot of shouting. Everyone is tightly packed, trying to keep in and not go too far wide, but I'm losing rather than making ground. When we reach the seven-furlong marker I'm beginning to panic. I'm thinking: WE GOTTA GET OUTA HERE! I should be doing something about this but I'm stuck, one off the rail on the inside. I can't go round because that would take me six horses wide.

I'M IN THE SHIT!

I start niggling but no gaps are appearing, then just before the six-furlong pole there's a real schemozzle when one runner tries to move to the inside and tightens up those behind. Willie Ryan's horse Foyer hits the rail hard and bounces Willie out of the saddle. Suddenly there seems to be a bit more room. The runners fan out a little, and at last I'm able to start my move.

Coming down the hill I've got Erhaab on the rail, and at the five-furlong marker there's a gap on the inside: I can see ten lengths down it, so I ride him as hard as I can, urging him to pick up speed and get running. I'm screaming at all the others not to drop back on to the inner, and nearly scrape the rail myself. I'm a fifty-one-year-old jockey going through the eye of a needle and my adrenalin is really flowing – I'm ready to jump off a cliff. I'm so high I could do anything, and luckily the gaps keep opening. I'm still shouting and screaming, and the other jockeys help by holding their horses off the rail as I'm going past them so quickly. Erhaab's adrenalin must be high as well. He's really running by now, and as I keep stoking up his momentum he must be thinking: BLOODY HELL! HOW DO WE GET OUT OF THIS?

'Bloody hell! How do we get out of this?'

Ever Ready Derby

Epsom, 1 June 1994	$1\frac{1}{2}$ miles	
1 ERHAAB	W. Carson	7–2 fav
2 King's Theatre	M. J. Kinane	14–1
3 Colonel Collins	J. Reid	10–1

Also ran: Mister Baileys (4th), Khamaseen, Pencader, Golden Ball, Just Happy, Star Selection, Linney Head, Ionio, Chocolat De Meguro, Weigh Anchor, Wishing, Party Season, Jabaroot, Waiting, Chickawicka, Sunshack, The Flying Phantom, Broadway Flyer, Darkwood Bay, Colonel Colt, Plato's Republic, Foyer

25 ran $1\frac{1}{4}$ lengths, $1\frac{1}{2}$ lengths

When we reach Tattenham Corner I look ahead. F***ING HELL! Mister Baileys seems like he's twenty-five lengths in front of me. I'll never catch him. But the pace has been so furious that the Guineas winner cannot sustain his speed, and halfway up the straight starts to fade rapidly, swamped by Colonel Collins and King's Theatre. I keep pumping away but it's a case of the leaders stopping, not of my horse accelerating. Erhaab is going the same pace and catching the leaders, but he's hanging on the rail, leaning on it for help, as if something is not quite right with him. I keep him on the rail until a furlong out, then drag him to the outside to pass Colonel Collins and King's Theatre. We win by a length and a quarter . . .

I don't think I've ever been so exhausted after a race. Perhaps it was my age. Normally after winning a race like that my adrenalin would still be flowing, but for some reason I felt down. Maybe I frightened myself riding that way, throwing caution to the wind. It could have gone horribly wrong, and if one horse had moved back on to the rail as we were making our move Erhaab would never have been heard of. But when Bruce Raymond told me, 'I can't believe you've won – what a ride!', that reaction from an old sweat jockey meant a great deal to me. If Bruce said that, it must have been good. Feeling absolutely drained, I pulled up and took Erhaab – himself so knackered that he could hardly raise a canter – back towards the unsaddling enclosure. Photographer Gerry Cranham asked me to wave, but I barely had the strength to lift my arm.

Ten minutes later I was OK, and able to reflect a little on the race. Erhaab could so easily have been beaten: if I'd hustled him early on or if he'd encountered trouble in running he would not have won. But he never got bumped once, and he went through the eye of the needle without flinching.

Derby winners have to be brave or brilliant. Shergar was so brilliant he didn't need to be brave. I wouldn't call Nashwan a brave horse, but he was certainly brilliant. Troy was both – the sort of horse to go to war with when the bullets are flying. Erhaab may have had something wrong with him before the Derby, and may have been in some pain during the race. He never really had the chance subsequently to show whether he was brilliant, but on Derby Day he was certainly brave. **"**

Pat Eddery

Grundy in the King George VI and Queen Elizabeth Diamond Stakes, Ascot, 26 July 1975

PAT EDDERY WAS BRED TO BE A JOCKEY. His father Jimmy had ridden Panaslipper to come second to Phil Drake in the 1955 Epsom Derby before winning the Irish equivalent at The Curragh, and it was near that racecourse that his son Pat, fifth of twelve surviving children, was born on 18 March 1952. Pat's mother Josephine was the daughter of a jockey, Jack Moylan, with whom Jimmy Eddery had dead-heated in the 1944 Irish Two Thousand Guineas.

At the age of thirteen Pat was apprenticed to Seamus McGrath (for whose stable his father rode), and in 1967 moved to England to serve the rest of his apprenticeship with Frenchie Nicholson. He rode his first winner at the age of seventeen on Alvaro at Epsom on 24 April 1969 and his first Royal Ascot winner, Sky Rocket in the Wokingham Handicap, later the same season. At Haydock Park on 22 August 1970 he achieved the remarkable feat for an apprentice – indeed, for any jockey – of riding five winners in the same day for five different trainers, and in 1971 was champion apprentice. In 1972 he joined trainer Peter Walwyn in Lambourn, and it was for Walwyn that he rode his first winner of an English Classic: Polygamy in the 1974 Oaks.

The same season saw Eddery champion jockey for the first time, at twenty-two years of age the youngest rider to win the title since Gordon Richards in 1925, and 1975 brought him his first Derby, on Grundy. Further triumphs in the premier Classic came on Golden Fleece in 1982 and Quest For Fame in 1990.

Pat Eddery won his first Prix de l'Arc de Triomphe on Detroit in 1980, and later in the 1980s took the Arc three years running: on Rainbow Quest in 1985, Dancing Brave in 1986 and Trempolino in 1987. His position as one of the finest jockeys on the international stage was highlighted by Breeders' Cup victories on Pebbles in the 1985 Turf and Sheikh Albadou in the 1991 Sprint.

By the start of the 1996 season Pat Eddery had been champion jockey in Great Britain on ten occasions, just one fewer than Lester Piggott – and in 1982 he was champion in

Ireland, where he had succeeded Piggott as stable jockey to Vincent O'Brien. For O'Brien he rode dozens of big winners, but ironically the partnership is perhaps best remembered for a defeat – that of El Gran Senor by Secreto in the 1984 Derby.

The 1990 season saw Eddery amass a domestic total of 209 winners, which made him the first Flat jockey since Gordon Richards in 1952 to pass 200. He rode the 3,000th winner of his career in July 1991 and by the beginning of 1996 was fourth in the list of winning-most British-based jockeys, behind Richards, Piggott and Carson.

Enough of the stats. What about the horses?

66 I've been privileged to ride some great horses. Pebbles was the finest filly; but for the very best among the colts I find it difficult to choose between Dancing Brave, El Gran Senor and Golden Fleece.

They were all very different. Golden Fleece had so much brilliance but was not able to run after the Derby and thus never received the credit he deserved. Dancing Brave and El Gran Senor were superb rides, but Golden Fleece could be very tricky. He was a great big horse who always wanted to run away with me in a race, and the only time I ever got him to settle was in the Derby. We took him over to Epsom a few days before and worked out a routine. The first morning I walked him across to the mile-and-a-half start, walked him two furlongs down the track, hack cantered down to the seven-furlong pole, then walked him back to the stables. The next morning he was due to work, so I walked him about a furlong up from the Derby start, then jumped off. He needed to learn to relax, and this routine did the trick. In the Derby he jumped off well, didn't pull, and I deliberately didn't put him in the race early on in case he got too keen. He stayed at the back, but I knew I had to wait and wait, and we were still among the back markers rounding Tattenham Corner. Halfway up the straight I pulled him out and he made up about ten lengths in half a furlong. He felt like a fantastic horse that day, but Vincent said he wasn't right. It was tragic that Golden Fleece could never run again and prove how good he was.

In the Derby two years later El Gran Senor looked to be absolutely hacking up, and was then worried out of it by Secreto, who beat him a short head. There was a great deal of discussion about why El Gran Senor was beaten: many people said I should have kicked on once we'd taken the lead, but as far as I'm concerned it was quite the opposite – I simply got there too soon. I was tracking Claude Monet, but when he folded up suddenly after swallowing a clod of earth El Gran Senor was left in front much too early. It was just one of those things. When I rode El Gran Senor in the Irish Derby I put him there right on the line, which was the way to do it. He may not have won at Epsom, but he was certainly a great horse.

So, of course, was Dancing Brave, but like many other great horses he tended to stop once he hit the front – a fact they omitted to tell me the first time I rode him, in the King George at Ascot. I waited until the final furlong, shot past Shardari – then he all but pulled up dead on me. So I knew before the Arc that I had to wait and wait, that I had to be the last to challenge. In a race with so many Group One winners in the field this was easier said than done, but I knew that I just had to be last, so bided my time until I had them all – Bering, Triptych, Shardari, Darara, Shahrastani and the rest – in my sights, then stoked Dancing Brave up, got him going up the centre of the track, and picked them off. That was a great feeling.

Pebbles winning the Breeders' Cup Turf at Aqueduct in 1985 was very exciting. I dropped her right out, got a good run down the back straight, had her on the fence turning into the straight, and then as the leaders ran wide off the final bend was able to push her through the gap. She showed a great turn of foot and stayed on wonderfully well to hold off Steve Cauthen on Strawberry Road.

That was her only race over a mile and a half. Her best trip was certainly ten furlongs, and her greatest race at that distance was the one before the Breeders' Cup, the Champion Stakes in October 1985, when she was opposed by the likes of Slip Anchor and Commanche Run. I'd not ridden her before, but as Steve Cauthen – who had won the Eclipse on her back in July, since when she hadn't run – would be on Slip Anchor, I asked Clive Brittain for the mount. After consulting her owner Sheikh Mohammed he confirmed that I could ride, and during the week before the race I rode her work at Newmarket. She did not go particularly well in that gallop, but on Champion Stakes day she was spot-on, to the extent that she got quite worked up, messing about and throwing herself all over the place. I got off her at the start and she started to calm down, then in the race ran quite brilliantly. I kept her at the back to get her relaxed, then asked her to move up a little bit. She went through the field so easily I had to take a pull, and she just cruised past the others on the snaffle and won easing down. When you consider the quality of the opposition, this was a sensational performance.

And yet the race of my life has to be the obvious one – Grundy in the 1975 King George. There was such a marvellous build-up, the field was so strong, and the race itself was unforgettable.

Still only twenty-three, I'd won my first jockeys' title the season before, and to get a great horse like Grundy so early in my riding career was a tremendous boost. His first outing as a two-year-old was in a maiden at Ascot in July 1974. Peter Walwyn had two in the race – Grundy and No Alimony – and we weren't sure from their work at home which was the better. I opted to ride Grundy, and although he ran a little green we won easily by two lengths from No Alimony, a very satisfactory start to his career. The following month he won at Kempton, and then went to Doncaster and landed the Champagne Stakes before turning in a marvellous performance to win the Dewhurst Stakes by six lengths from Steel Heart. Four races as a juvenile, four wins.

The following spring he was just about ready to run when another horse kicked him in the head while they were trotting round the covered ride before going out on the gallops. He got over this, but after his first piece of work following the incident bled through his nose – alarming at the time, but he was fine when he next worked and the immediate panic was over. But it was still essential to get a race into him before his major early-season target, the Two Thousand Guineas, so we ran him in the Greenham

'The race itself was unforgettable'

49

Stakes at Newbury. He was beaten by Mark Anthony, but we weren't too disappointed as we knew Grundy would come on a great deal for the race.

The start of the Two Thousand Guineas was disrupted by a demonstration of striking stable lads, and we actually set off from in front of the stalls, thus making the race short of its official distance of a mile. This did not suit Grundy, and he was outpaced by a very speedy horse in Bolkonski – though the pair finished well clear of the rest. Grundy then went to The Curragh for the Irish Two Thousand Guineas, as much as anything to reassure us that he was good enough and had enough potential stamina to go for the Derby. He won going away, and Epsom would be the next stop.

Grundy and Bustino head to head.

In many ways Grundy appealed as the ideal Derby horse. Although he was of that flashy chestnut colour which does not please some, he was a beautifully balanced little colt – compact and neat, and blessed with a very good temperament and a serious turn of foot. Sure enough, he went round Epsom like a dream and bolted up by three lengths from the French filly Nobiliary. He then cruised home in the Irish Derby, and our thoughts turned to Ascot.

That year's King George was a classic confrontation between the generations. Grundy was clearly the top three-year-old in the land, and Bustino, winner of the St Leger in 1974 and of the Coronation Cup on his only outing to date in 1975, the top four-year-old. In addition, the field contained the great French mare Dahlia, winner of the King George in 1973 and 1974 and still the only dual winner of the race; Star Appeal, who had won the Eclipse and would go on to land the Arc; the filly Dibidale, winner of the Irish Oaks in 1974 and so unlucky in the Oaks itself when her saddle slipped close home; the three-year-old Libra's Rib, winner of the King Edward VII Stakes at Royal Ascot; and three more very strong French challengers in Ashmore, On My Way and Card King.

The two other runners, both 500–1 outsiders, held the key to the race. Kinglet and Highest, both like Bustino owned by Lady Beaverbrook and trained by Dick Hern, were there as pacemakers. Dick Hern was convinced that Grundy would not truly stay the mile and a half and was determined to exploit Bustino's undoubted strength – stamina – by ensuring a strong gallop. Bustino's usual pacemaker was Riboson, who had done his job so well in the 1974 St Leger that he stayed on to finish third, but he was injured at the time of the King George, so the novel plan was hatched to use two stable companions – a miler and a stayer – to force the pace.

It was no surprise that the Bustino team should seek to capitalise on their horse's strength, but the pace which those two set from the start was staggering. I'd expected a good mile-and-a-half clip early on. Instead we hammered down from the start to Swinley Bottom like six-furlong sprinters – it was amazing! Highest led us for the first half mile or so, with Kinglet second and Bustino third. I was in fourth, with Star Appeal upsides. At Swinley Bottom, Star Appeal went by me as Highest gave up the ghost and the stayer Kinglet took up the running, while I stayed tracking Joe Mercer on Bustino. Kinglet led for most of the long stretch out of Swinley Bottom until Bustino took it up approaching the home straight. With Grundy already off the bridle, I desperately tried to keep him in my sights, thinking: I'd better get after him. But I just couldn't go with him: he was gone – three or four lengths up – and kept on finding more, and it was well into the straight before I thought I'd reach him. Halfway up the straight I started to come alongside him, a furlong out I thought: I've got you! I just headed him and felt that we'd go on for a hard-fought but decisive victory, then – shit! – those green and brown colours appeared on the inside again. That tough old bugger was fighting back!

Grundy was not a big horse – Bustino was a size larger – but was endowed with tremendous guts and honesty, and now his bravery saw him

King George VI and Queen Elizabeth Diamond Stakes

Ascot, 26 July 1975		$1\frac{1}{2}$ miles	
1 GRUNDY	Pat Eddery		4–5 fav
2 Bustino	J. Mercer		4–1
3 Dahlia	L. Piggott		6–1

Also ran: On My Way (4th), Card King, Ashmore, Dibidale, Libra's Rib, Star Appeal, Kinglet, Highest

11 ran	$\frac{1}{2}$ length, 5 lengths

home. He just kept going and hung on through the final half furlong as Bustino finally cracked. We got there by half a length, with Dahlia five lengths back in third.

Four or five strides after the line Grundy wobbled to a halt. He was an amazingly tough racehorse but that race bottomed him, and he was so tired that I thought for a moment I'd have to get off him to enable him to walk into the unsaddling enclosure. In the event he managed it all right, but he was completely drained.

He seemed to have recovered and we aimed him at the Benson and Hedges Gold Cup at York in August. I did not ride him in between the two races, but Matt McCormack, his usual work rider, was convinced that he was as good as ever. On the day of the race Grundy looked marvellous and we felt confident, but he ran very flat. From about half a mile out I knew that he had gone, and that the Ascot race had left its mark, if not physically then certainly mentally.

He never raced again, but that day at Ascot he was a lion of a horse. His meeting with another lion produced one of the greatest races of all. **"**

Ron Barry

Grand Canyon in the Colonial Cup, Camden, South Carolina, 27 November 1976

'HE WAS AS HARD AS NAILS, WOULD TAKE any ride and was an exceptionally good rider with a style all his own.'

There's nothing like the opinion of a fellow professional to gauge the true worth of any top sportsman, and that tribute from Terry Biddlecombe has the authority of one former champion jump jockey saluting another – Ron Barry. Variously known as 'Big Ron' and 'King of the Chat' – both epithets applied for obvious reasons – Ron Barry was one of the finest jump jockeys of his era, famed for his strength, fearlessness and irrepressible bonhomie in and out of the saddle.

Ron Barry was born on 28 February 1943 in County Limerick, where from an early age he rode ponies around his parents'

farm. He served his apprenticeship with trainer Tommy Shaw, then moved to Britain, riding his first winner – Final Approach in a novice hurdle – at Ayr on 19 October 1964, and gradually worked his way to the top. He took his first jockeys' championship in 1972–3, with the then record total of 125 winners, and a second title the following season. He retired in 1983.

The horse with whom Big Ron is most readily associated is his 1973 Cheltenham Gold Cup winner The Dikler, as memorable a chaser as any to have raced since Arkle. A huge, strapping bay horse with a large white blaze and a serious attitude problem – on first seeing the horse, Ron Barry described him as 'an enormous, powerful beast' – The Dikler was a standing dish in the big staying chases in the 1970s. He won the King George VI Chase (ridden by Barry Brogan) in 1971 and the Whitbread Gold Cup (ridden by Ron Barry) on the disqualification of Proud Tarquin and John Oaksey in 1975, and ran in the Cheltenham Gold Cup for seven consecutive years: on three of those occasions he was ridden by Ron Barry.

Despite his regular appearances in the line-up for big races, the Champion Hurdle eluded Ron, who came closest when second to Comedy Of Errors on Easby Abbey in 1973, and he was never placed in the Grand National, though his first experience of the race in 1971 brought him 'a dream of a ride'.

" I was at Wolverhampton a few weeks before the National, and my guv'nor Gordon Richards pointed out to me Jack O'Donaghue, who had trained Nickel Coin to win the race in 1951: 'There's the man you want to speak to about how to ride the National. Go and have a word with him.' I trailed him all day trying to get a word, but he was too busy. So I hung around until after the last race, when I managed to nab him in the bar.

'Mr O'Donaghue, the boss said I should have a word with you about how to ride Liverpool.'

'Yes, son, of course.'

'So what's the best way to do it?'

He thought for a minute, then:

'The only advice I can give you is – have three or four large brandies before you start!'

I rode Sandy Sprite, a mare trained by John Edwards, and we were well in front with two to jump. She'd been brilliant through the race, jumping from fence to fence, and was absolutely cantering coming over the Melling Road, but broke down after the second last, and could only hobble home to finish fifth behind Specify.

The two best horses I rode have to be Playlord and The Dikler. Playlord, who was Gordon Richards's first really decent horse, was temperamental but very classy: he could have won the Gold Cup with better luck – he was third to What A Myth in 1969 – and we won the 1969 Scottish National under

After the last, Ron Barry and Grand Canyon (sheepskin noseband) head for home from the grey Fire Control. Lanzarote, who finished fourth, is on the left.

twelve stone, but his greatest moment with me was when he won the Great Yorkshire Chase earlier that season, going clear of a good field to win by seven lengths from Domacorn. My uncle said it looked like a cowboy film, with the baddie way out in front and the posse vainly chasing from behind!

The Dikler was like Playlord in that he was tremendously strong and a prodigious jumper. I got the ride in the 1973 Cheltenham Gold Cup as his usual partners Willie Robinson and Barry Brogan had both retired, and Terry Biddlecombe suggested to his trainer Fulke Walwyn that I might be a suitable rider for him; so I went down to Lambourn before the Gold Cup to get to know him. I've always enjoyed a challenge, and riding The Dikler was certainly that. I had never sat on such a powerful horse: he was unbelievably strong.

Not long before the big Cheltenham meeting I had broken my collarbone, and with a couple of days to go it was still very sore. It seemed to me that my biggest problem on Gold Cup day would not be the hot favourite Pendil, trained by Fred Winter and ridden by Richard Pitman, but getting The Dikler down to the start: how was I going to restrain him in my state? In the event he cantered down sweetly, and once the race started the leaders went off so fast that he just dropped the bit, went to sleep and ambled away: a three-year-old child could have ridden him. He lobbed along for the first circuit and a half, gave himself his customary breather, then coming down the hill towards the home straight I tried to get him into the race. I was tracking Terry Biddlecombe on Charlie Potheen, who started to hang towards the rail, so had to check and move outside him, which in the circumstances was probably just as well, as it meant we didn't come too soon to tackle Pendil, who looked to be cantering going to the last. Pendil jumped it well but The Dikler put in a mighty leap, landed galloping and set off up the run-in after him. He made up ground hand over fist and as Pendil faltered I knew we'd get there. We did, but only just, reaching Pendil close home and resisting his late rally to win by a short head.

I had some great times with The Dikler. In terms of sheer power he was certainly the most exciting horse I ever rode: sitting on him, you felt like you had a mile of horse in front of you. Despite his phenomenal strength, the ideal way to ride him was to get him to drop the bit and settle: put him in behind a wall of horses and persuade him to turn off. The flaw in this plan was that he was such a wonderful jumper that he'd make two lengths in the air and before you knew it you were up their backsides again.

But for the race of my life I think that the 1973 Gold Cup would just be pipped by my win in the 1976 Colonial Cup in Camden, South Carolina, on Grand Canyon.

The New Zealand-bred Grand Canyon, trained by Derek Kent, was a real globe-trotter who that season raced in Italy, France, the USA, England and Ireland. In those days it was pretty unusual for hurdlers or chasers to campaign in the USA, and the Colonial Cup, a famous race run in a wonderfully informal atmosphere which made it somewhat like a glorified point-to-point, had never been won by a foreign horse.

I rode Grand Canyon in his race before Camden, a hurdle at Newbury,

'The days leading up to the race saw breakfast parties merge into lunch parties, lunch parties into dinner parties, dinner parties into the next day's breakfast parties...'

Colonial Cup

Camden, South Carolina, 27 November 1976   *2 miles 6 furlongs*

1 GRAND CANYON	R. Barry	
2 Fire Control	D. Small	
3 Crag's Corner	M. Walsh	

[no betting officially returned]

Also ran: Lanzarote (4th), Straight And True, Happy Intellectual, Juggernaut II, Casamayor, The Bo-Weevil, Irish Fashion, Beau Dad, Cyano Mist, Life's Illusion, Arctic Joe, Tor's Lib, Tan Jay

16 ran $\frac{1}{2}$ *length,* $2\frac{1}{2}$ *lengths*

and he won easily, so I crossed the Atlantic in confident mood. This horse could really gallop, and as far as I was concerned there was nothing in the world that could go with him. He was a hurdler, but the fences on the Colonial Cup course were much smaller versions of our chase fences, and jumping would be no problem. When I arrived in South Carolina and saw some recordings of previous races, though, I wasn't so sure: they clearly went one hell of a lick there, and my confidence evaporated. No longer did my horse look like a certainty – more like a 25–1 shot!

My spirits were considerably raised, however, by the level of hospitality on offer during Colonial Cup week. This was one of the great jamborees of American steeplechasing, and the days leading up to the race saw breakfast parties merge into lunch parties, lunch parties into dinner parties, dinner parties into the next day's breakfast parties . . .

On the day, there was plenty of razzmatazz leading up to the race itself, with parades and bands, and Grand Canyon got himself very agitated. The quality of the opposition was high, the field including most of the top American chasers – whom I had seen not long before when riding at Belmont Park, and who seemed to give Grand Canyon little to worry about – as well as some very good horses from our side of the Atlantic, including the 1974 Champion Hurdler Lanzarote, just embarking on a chasing career, and Irish Fashion, on whom I had won the Schweppes Gold Trophy at Newbury that spring.

A tearaway pace was set through the first mile of the race by Life's Illusion, and despite my confidence in Grand Canyon's galloping powers I had no inclination to take this horse on, even when he stretched his lead to fifteen or twenty lengths. My fellow fought for his head and put in a couple of hairy jumps, then moved up gradually so that at the fifth from home we took up the running, only for Life's Illusion to come back upsides after

Grand Canyon made another error. Approaching the third last the other horse started to fade rapidly and we went on, going perhaps two or three lengths up. I was beginning to feel sure that we'd win, then all of a sudden other horses started coming at me left, right and centre. Two out a grey horse named Fire Control was all but upsides, and Lanzarote was getting closer, but Grand Canyon put in a great leap which gave him the advantage he needed, and he held off Fire Control over the last and was still half a length to the good at the post. Lanzarote was fourth.

The rider of Fire Control lodged an objection against me on the grounds of interference – I had not felt or noticed anything untoward – but the result was allowed to stand. Which is just as well, as Grand Canyon thus became the first overseas-trained horse to win the Colonial Cup, and the profile of the race was significantly increased.

If the run-up to the race had been one big party, the post-race celebration was something else! Luckily my memory of it is hazy . . .

Grand Canyon missed the Colonial Cup the following year but we were back in Camden in 1978, winning again and breaking his own course record set in 1976. On his day he was an exhilarating ride – and I had a few of those in my riding years . . . **99**

Both Grand Canyon and his rider found new careers after retirement. The horse went into the Household Cavalry, where he was a less than unqualified success, habits acquired as a racehorse proving difficult to shake off during ceremonial duties. Ron Barry found it easier to adjust, and in 1987 became the Jockey Club's Inspector of Courses on the northern circuit, a role for which he was eminently well qualified by one of the most distinguished and exciting careers of recent memory.

Jonjo O'Neill

Dawn Run in the Tote Cheltenham Gold Cup, Cheltenham, 13 March 1986

LIKE ALL SPORTS, HORSE RACING HAS ITS SELECT band of leading participants who are instantly identified by a Christian name: Gordon, for example, Lester, Frankie – and Jonjo.

Jonjo O'Neill has won the affection of the racing public as much through his indefatigable cheerfulness, good humour and courage – qualities which not only served him well in racing but also saw him fight cancer and win – as through the skills which made him twice champion jump jockey and later a top trainer.

John Joe O'Neill was born in County Cork on 13 April 1952. He served his apprenticeship with Michael Connolly at The Curragh, and rode his first winner, Lana, when dead-heating in a Flat race at the local track on 9 September 1970. He moved to England in 1973, joined Gordon Richards's stable at Penrith, and soon made his presence felt at the highest level of the sport. In the 1977–8 season he was champion jockey for the first time, with the then record total of 149 winners, and gained a second championship in 1979–80.

Jonjo never won the Grand National (indeed, he never got round in the race), but he struck twice in each of the other two legs of jump racing's Big Three: the Champion Hurdle on Sea Pigeon in 1980 and Dawn Run in 1984, and the Cheltenham Gold Cup on Alverton in 1979 and Dawn Run in 1986. On the great Sea Pigeon he won fifteen races, including four on the Flat – notably a famous short-head victory over Donegal Prince in the 1979 Ebor Handicap. Another famous jumper he partnered regularly was Night Nurse, on whom he landed one hurdle and five chases.

Jonjo O'Neill retired from the saddle at the end of April 1986 to take up a training career which has brought him success at the top level both on the Flat – his Gipsy Fiddler won the Windsor Castle Stakes at Royal Ascot in 1990 – and over jumps, taking the Coral Golden Hurdle Final at the 1991 Cheltenham Festival (his first Festival winner) with Danny Connors.

In all he rode 885 winners in Britain. No prizes for guessing which of those was the race of his life.

"For sheer ability, Sea Pigeon was certainly the best horse I ever rode. He had masses of class and tremendous speed, and wanted very little interference from his jockey: the less you did on him, the better he was.

Dawn Run was the opposite. She was very moody, and for me at least not a very comfortable ride: I never felt that I really fitted into her neatly and tidily, but we had some wonderful moments together, and her victory in the 1986 Cheltenham Gold Cup has to be the greatest day of my riding life.

I first rode Dawn Run in the V.A.T. Watkins Hurdle at Ascot in November 1983, by which time, after a highly successful 1982–3 campaign, she was hotly fancied for the 1984 Champion Hurdle. At Ascot she had to fight very hard to beat Amarach by a short head, and was then beaten by Boreen Deas – to whom she was conceding lumps of weight – at Naas. In her next race, the Christmas Hurdle at Kempton Park, she narrowly defeated the reigning champion Gaye Brief. She went on to beat Cima in the Champion Hurdle, but I was injured on the first day of the Liverpool Grand National meeting and Tony Mullins rode her to win the Aintree Hurdle on National Day and later the Prix la Barka and the Grande Course de Haies at Auteuil.

The following season she went chasing, winning on her debut at Navan before being sidelined by a leg injury. Still Tony's ride, she reappeared in December 1985 to win chases at Punchestown and Leopardstown, and in January 1986 went to Cheltenham for her pre-Gold Cup race, only to make such an almighty blunder at the last open ditch that poor Tony had no chance of staying on board.

Dawn Run's owner Mrs Charmian Hill had herself won a bumper at Tralee on Dawn Run at the age of sixty-three and considered she knew all there was to know about riding the mare. She decided Tony had to be replaced again, and when Paddy Mullins phoned to ask if I could take over the ride, I readily agreed.

I went over to school her at Gowran Park, not far from Paddy's yard. This was the first time I'd sat on her since the Champion Hurdle nearly two years earlier, and I soon realised that the major threat to her Gold Cup chance was her jumping. She was desperate – couldn't jump a twig! Possibly because she had been hurdling for so long, she was having trouble getting the hang of taking fences. A big, long-striding mare, she was fantastic at flying a hurdle and could be brilliant when meeting a fence right, but she had little clue about adjusting herself: she would never be a natural over the larger obstacles. After that schooling session at Gowran Park some of the boys asked me about her Gold Cup chances: never mind winning, I told them, she shouldn't have been entered!

With her immediate pre-Cheltenham races lost to the weather, we thought we'd better school her again, so took her to Punchestown. At Gowran Park she had been schooled on her own, which I felt may not have helped, so we had a stablemate with her at Punchestown, and with the Gold Cup field taking shape it was time to start thinking about our tactics. Looking at the entries for the big race, it was clear that the field could

'We went to the first like shit off a shovel'

59

contain several pacemakers – among them horses of the calibre of Run And Skip and Cybrandian. I thought to myself: none of those would have the speed to win a Champion Hurdle, and I could probably drop Dawn Run right out of it, then go on and win the race whenever I wanted. All I needed to do was confirm that she was happy being dropped out. The school at Punchestown soon put me right. When I dropped her in behind the other horse – ridden by Tony – I just couldn't get her out. She wouldn't raise a gallop. After that I went hell for leather at the fences with her, and she pinged them beautifully. The conclusion was obvious. Speed or no speed, I would have no alternative at Cheltenham but to go on, and the Gold Cup tactic was simple: get in front and stay there.

Bedlam as Jonjo O'Neill and Dawn Run return to unsaddle.

Dawn Run was favourite for the Gold Cup at 15–8, with 1985 winner Forgive'N Forget 7–2, Combs Ditch 9–2, Run And Skip 15–2 and Wayward Lad 8–1. I knew we had a favourite's chance – she was clearly the best horse in the race – but my worry was still that her jumping might be found out at that level. If I could just get her round she would win – simple as that!

In the paddock beforehand I felt confident, a feeling increased by Paddy Mullins's simple statement: 'The mare is well. You know yourself what to do.' That was the extent of his riding orders, which suited me fine.

At the start I was trying to keep an eye on the other front-runners, thinking: I've got to get to the inner, I need to be on the inner. But I couldn't get there, so I let Dawn Run stand side on across the starting tape, pleading with the starter: 'Sir, I can't get out, you'll have to send them back!' He did so, I nipped over to the inside, and then we were off.

We went to the first like shit off a shovel. Coming to the fence Dawn Run was spot-on, but was being distracted by the cheering: she always reacted to the crowd, and what's more there were people lining the approach to the first and she wanted to take a good look at them. I roared at her to get her attention, to try to keep her concentration on the fence, but her mind wasn't fully on the job and she half hurdled it, clipping the top and nodding on landing. My heart went to my knees, but she picked her feet up and kept galloping on, pinged the second, and then settled down in the lead, with Steve Smith Eccles and Run And Skip keeping us close company.

We went a tremendous gallop all the way, and as we passed the stands at the end of the first circuit I wanted to give her a breather. But Run And Skip was always chasing us along and I couldn't let up and risk her getting behind, so had to keep after her. As we set out on the second circuit I was still full of hope, but she dropped her hind legs in the water, just the sort of setback I didn't need when I was looking for the opportunity to give her a breather. Steve on Run And Skip was kicking on so I had to get the mare back upsides, and I found myself thinking that if I could get her over the open ditch at the top of the hill – where she had unshipped Tony – she would win. We were going so fast that surely nothing could come and take us from behind, as long as we kept up this gallop and gave nothing away through jumping mistakes.

She jumped the ditch well enough, but the next she missed completely, and Run And Skip went past, moved in towards the rail and almost cut off her nose. I had to drag her out from behind him to give her as much daylight as possible. I thought: if she misses the next, that's it – but she flew it and Run And Skip missed, and I was back in front again, charging down the hill and sure we would win. Still I needed to give her a chance by taking a breather, but there was little time. She pinged the third last just behind Run And Skip and the pair of us swept into the straight with Wayward Lad and Forgive'N Forget coming into contention.

I needed a good jump at the second last and just before the fence gave her a slap down the neck. She flew it – but as I landed, to my complete astonishment, the others went by me. I couldn't believe it! For an instant I thought I was beaten – she'd done everything I asked her but that was it,

Tote Cheltenham Gold Cup

Cheltenham, 13 March 1986	$3\frac{1}{4}$ miles	
1 DAWN RUN	J. J. O'Neill	15–8 fav
2 Wayward Lad	G. Bradley	8–1
3 Forgive'N Forget	M. Dwyer	7–2

Also ran: Run And Skip (4th), Righthand Man, Observe, Combs Ditch, Earls Brig, Von Trappe, Castle Andrea, Cybrandian

11 ran	1 length, $2\frac{1}{2}$ lengths

she was beat. The only thing I hadn't done was give her a breather, so I sat up for a moment and eased off – and fifty yards off the last fence she started to pick up again. She was revved up and so was I, and we went for the last. For a moment I had it in mind to ask her for a big one, but I left her alone and she picked up just as she had done at the second last.

We landed in third behind Wayward Lad and Forgive'N Forget, and I knew then that we would not get beaten. I'd ridden Wayward Lad in the Gold Cup three years before, and knew that, fine horse as he was, he didn't get this trip. Forgive'N Forget didn't have the bottle, but Dawn Run did – and so did I! Wayward Lad started hanging towards the left-hand rail, a clear sign that he'd come to the end of his tether. That left Forgive'N Forget in front, but he was not the sort to run to the line, so I gave Dawn Run a few clouts, knowing she would rally and stay on, and she did just that, clawing her way back up the centre of the track to collar Wayward Lad and go on to win by a length.

The minute she passed the line those old ears pricked up and I knew that again she was not taking notice of anything except the noise of the crowd. What a noise it was! As we walked past the stands the cheering swept down and engulfed us. It was just amazing, a fitting greeting for the first horse ever to have won the Champion Hurdle and the Gold Cup. The cheering got stronger and stronger as we were led in, and it seemed it would go on for ever. There was bedlam when we finally reached the paddock, and for a moment it looked as if Dawn Run and I were going to be swept into the weighing-room.

After unsaddling and weighing in I returned to the continuing mayhem, where in the crush I found Tony Mullins, who had done so much to make Dawn Run the great racehorse she was, and hoisted him up on to my shoulders. It was all glorious chaos, fitting recognition of a unique achievement by the mare.

Dawn Run's next race was at the beginning of April at Liverpool. She was very hyped up going down to the start, set off like a bat out of hell and was meeting the first spot-on, ears pricked – but she paid not the slightest attention to my asking her to jump it. She went straight through the fence, and that was that.

I did not ride her again, and announced my retirement later that month. Tony Mullins was reunited with her for her match against Buck House at Punchestown (which she won) and the Prix la Barka at Auteuil (in which she was second), only to be removed again for the Grande Course de Haies in favour of French jockey Michel Chirol. The mare was killed instantly when breaking her neck in a fall at the fifth last. She was only eight years old.

I remember once discussing her quality with Paddy Mullins. She was not obviously brilliant in the way that a horse like Sea Pigeon was, so what was it that made her so special? Said Paddy, 'She just keeps doing it,' and he was right. In all honesty, she ran much sweeter for Tony than for me: they just suited each other, and it was his bad luck that he did not keep the ride. She was a funny old thing – but I was glad to get on her! 99

Joe Mercer

Bustino in the King George VI and Queen Elizabeth Diamond Stakes, Ascot, 26 July 1975

WHEN JOE MERCER RETIRED FROM THE saddle after riding Bold Rex to victory in the November Handicap at Doncaster in 1985, his 2,810 domestic winners made him the fourth most successful Flat jockey in British racing history. His total has since been passed by both Willie Carson and Pat Eddery, but the memory of Mercer's skills remains bright: the quintessence of the stylish and balanced rider, sympathetic yet strong, a fine judge of pace and an exceptional horseman.

Joe Mercer was born on 25 October 1934, and rode his first winner at the age of fifteen: Eldoret at Bath on 13 September 1950. After an apprenticeship to Major Frederick Sneyd, under whose care he was champion apprentice in 1952, he became retained jockey to Jack Colling, for whom the following year (when he was again champion apprentice) he won his first English Classic, the Oaks on Ambiguity, at the tender age of eighteen.

Of the home Classics only the Derby eluded him: in addition to Ambiguity's Oaks he won the One Thousand Guineas on Highclere (1974) and One In A Million (1979), the Two Thousand Guineas on Brigadier Gerard (1971) and the St Leger on Provoke (1965), Bustino (1974), Light Cavalry (1980) and Cut Above (1981). Of those seven horses, five – Highclere, Brigadier Gerard, Provoke, Bustino and Cut Above – were trained by Dick Hern, for whom Mercer rode as stable jockey from 1962 to 1976; the other two, One In A Million and Light Cavalry, by Henry Cecil, his association with whom brought Mercer the riders' championship in 1979 at the age of forty-five.

Of all the great horses Joe Mercer rode through his distinguished career – including, alongside those Classic winners, the likes of the great miler Kris, Ascot Gold Cup winner Le Moss and Time Charter, on whom he won the 1983 King George at Ascot – one stands out: the mighty Brigadier Gerard, owned by John and Jean Hislop. Mercer rode The Brigadier in all his eighteen races and the pair tasted defeat just once – at the hands of Derby winner Roberto in the Benson and Hedges Gold Cup at York in 1972.

"The only reason The Brigadier got beaten by Roberto was that he was a sick horse at York, and never gave me the right feel in the race. Roberto went off like a bat out of hell, and halfway up the straight I tried to go past him, but whereas normally Brigadier Gerard would have gone on, that day he struggled and was clearly not himself. When he came into the unsaddling enclosure Buster Haslam, Dick Hern's travelling head lad, told the horse's lad not to let him get his head down. Later, walking back across the track towards the racecourse stables, The Brigadier lowered his head and mucus poured out of his nose. He was a sick horse that afternoon.

But what a horse he was! – good-looking, perfectly built, with a real character, what I'd call a knowing character.

In the spring of 1970 I returned to England after a little local difficulty with the customs authorities in India. Bobby Elliott, who was then a work rider for Major Hern, had written to me out there and said that the yard was full of cracking horses – and in particular one lovely two-year-old. This of course was The Brigadier, and when I returned to the yard I learned that he'd already made something of a reputation for himself. Everybody who had ridden him had been thrown off – just the once – as if he was saying: I'm the boss. The first time I rode him he did the same to me: he just whipped round, dropped his shoulder, dumped me on the ground and stood there looking at me: 'That's your place, down there!'

Unbeaten in four races at two, as a three-year-old he was a real racehorse, and one of the races of my life has to be the Two Thousand Guineas of 1971 when he came up against Mill Reef and the unbeaten My Swallow, who had both been brilliant two-year-olds and were preferred to my fellow in the betting. I settled in behind those two as they took each other on down the middle of the track, then tacked towards the stands side and went past to beat them easily. Some said the other two had cut each other's throats, but time was to prove Brigadier Gerard one of the very great milers, and it was a true result.

Each one of his eighteen races remains clearly etched in my mind, but the greatest race he ran for me was in the Prince of Wales Stakes at Royal Ascot in June 1972. On the Sunday before the meeting I'd been due to ride in Brussels, flying out in a light plane from Newbury. Shortly after take-off the plane hit overhead cables and crashed: tragically, the pilot was killed. I was thrown clear, but although my injuries were not severe I was fairly shaken by the incident. Not so shaken, though, that I could bear the thought of not partnering The Brigadier at the Royal meeting. I insisted I was fit enough to ride, but John Hislop wanted proof, and had Jimmy Lindley on standby just in case I could not convince him. The morning of the race I took a handful of painkillers to alleviate the ache from my cracked ribs before riding work, where they made me push a horse five furlongs up the gallop. I came through all right and John Hislop agreed to let me ride.

I'm convinced The Brigadier knew I wasn't right that day. It's as if he said to me before the race: 'Just sit tight, I'll get you through.' He looked after me – didn't pull, and absolutely sluiced in, beating Steel Pulse, who went on to win the Irish Derby, by five lengths. I managed to get off him in

Overleaf:
At the home turn in The Race of the Century: Bustino (Joe Mercer) has the lead on the inside from Grundy (Pat Eddery), with Dahlia (Lester Piggott) and Ashmore (Yves Saint-Martin) to Grundy's left. In the blinkers behind Bustino is Star Appeal (Greville Starkey), and on the wide outside is Libra's Rib (Frank Morby).

the winner's enclosure but didn't ride again that afternoon – in fact, I didn't ride again for another week.

Brigadier Gerard was a great illustration of class in a racehorse, never better demonstrated than when he won the 1972 King George at Ascot over a mile and a half. He was a brilliant miler and could get a mile and a quarter on his head, but no one knew how far his stamina would last. With a horse of that calibre you just have to take a chance, and John Hislop was very keen to try him over the trip, so we had a go. He managed it, but it was a combination of his guts and his class which got him home. Once he'd gone clear inside the final quarter mile he came to the limit of his stamina and started to roll around as Willie Carson on Parnell came at us. We had a right ding-dong, with The Brigadier one and a half lengths up on the line – and then came the stewards' enquiry. It seemed to go on for ages, but in the end we were OK. That race just showed what guts the horse had.

Talk of guts brings me to another King George, and what has to be *the* race of my life: the 1975 duel between Grundy and Bustino.

I rode Bustino in all his races. As a two-year-old in 1973 he ran just the once, in the Acomb Stakes at York. He came third, but it was an encouraging run, and as a son of that good racehorse Busted he could be expected to be a late developer. So Major Hern, having seen enough for that season, decided to put Bustino away until the following year.

As a three-year-old he had developed into a very fine individual indeed, with the most beautiful colour. I rode him in all his work that spring and got him used to dropping in behind other horses, teaching him to relax. His first race that year was at Sandown Park, where he beat Snow Knight in the Classic Trial, and he then defeated the same horse in the Derby Trial at Lingfield. Snow Knight was third that day but came good under Brian Taylor in the Derby, with Bustino back in fourth. My fellow would not have won, but I was a bit annoyed with myself for not being closer as I had kept him too far off the pace. He then ran second to Sagaro in France and won the Great Voltigeur at York before winning the St Leger in brilliant style.

Bustino was a true stayer. He did not have a real turn of foot, but had such stamina that he could quicken off a very fast pace so long as you did not ask him to accelerate suddenly.

Between three and four he took great strides in maturity, and on his reappearance in 1975 broke the course record at Epsom in the Coronation Cup, holding off Ashmore all the way up the straight and showing tremendous resolution: he just kept finding that bit more under pressure.

The day before that race Grundy, trained by Peter Walwyn and ridden by Pat Eddery, had won the Derby in great style, and afterwards had gone on to take the Irish Derby at The Curragh. So the scene was set for a clash between the generations – Grundy the top three-year-old, Bustino the top four-year-old – in the King George.

The key to Bustino at Ascot was how to make the most of his stamina and blunt Grundy's finishing speed, and we evolved a plan whereby we

'A great, great race, even though we'd lost'

King George VI and Queen Elizabeth Diamond Stakes

Ascot, 26 July 1975 $1\frac{1}{2}$ miles

1 Grundy	Pat Eddery	4–5 fav
2 BUSTINO	J. Mercer	4–1
3 Dahlia	L. Piggott	6–1

Also ran: On My Way (4th), Card King, Ashmore, Dibidale, Libra's Rib, Star Appeal, Kinglet, Highest

11 ran $\frac{1}{2}$ *length, 5 lengths*

would use not one but two pacemakers. We might even have used three had Riboson – who had played that role for Bustino so well in the 1974 St Leger that he had run on to finish third behind his stable-mate – not been injured, and in the end we decided to employ Highest and Kinglet, both owned like Bustino by Lady Beaverbrook. We wanted a truly run race, no messing around, to exploit any possible chink in Grundy's armour, and the strategy was that Highest would make the running for the first part of the race until giving way to Kinglet, who would if possible lead me well into the home turn.

Grundy and Bustino were not the only great horses in the field: the French mare Dahlia, who had won the King George the previous two years, was back again, and with Ashmore, second to Bustino at Epsom, up for another crack, it was a vintage line-up.

Highest, ridden by Frankie Durr, set off at a tremendous lick, but Bustino, far from dropping in behind, was running away until I got him covered up. After four furlongs Highest came to the end of his tether and Eric Eldin on Kinglet – a lovely little horse and a very good performer in his own right – took it up. By the time we got round Swinley Bottom, with about seven furlongs to go, Bustino was third or fourth, still running away. I would have loved Kinglet to have led me right into the home turn, but he could not keep up the pace. With about half a mile to go – and rapidly approaching the final bend – I was breathing down Kinglet's neck, and had no option but to take it up.

I was not at the time aware of where Grundy was – all I knew was that he was somewhere behind me! – and as far as I could tell from those around me I was the only one still on the bridle, so I kicked on into the bend and straightened up for the winning post. Bustino was a horse who would always keep on finding, finding, finding, and he responded with the courage that was his greatest quality. He hammered up the straight, and it was not until around the furlong marker that I became aware of the chestnut head with the crooked white blaze coming up the stands side. The battle was on.

Grundy got to me but he couldn't get past, and we knuckled down to the tussle I'd been expecting. I hit my fellow one smack. His tongue came out and he faltered as he changed his legs, but he kept on battling. It took a long time for Grundy to get to Bustino's head, but gradually the younger horse got the upper hand and started to go clear. Then for a moment Bustino started to get back: but I knew in my heart of hearts that he wouldn't make it, and his one final effort petered out as Grundy went clear to win by half a length.

We pulled up and walked back towards the unsaddling enclosure. Bustino was shattered – though not quite as shattered as the winner, who stood stock still for a while before mustering the strength even to walk back. A great, great race, even though we'd lost.

Afterwards Bustino was given four or five days off; there were thoughts of aiming him at the Prix de l'Arc de Triomphe, but the first time we cantered him after his break his tendon went, and there was no option but to retire him. Looking back on the King George, I'm convinced that the tendon gave when he changed his legs inside the final furlong, and that was the difference between winning and losing. That's not to take anything away from Grundy, who was a wonderful racehorse, but I'm convinced that Bustino lost because he broke down. He may have rapped himself: we'll just never know. 🙶

A small but telling additional piece of evidence to support the 1975 King George's reputation as The Race of the Century: it is the only race in this book to have been chosen by two jockeys.

Steve Cauthen

Affirmed in the Belmont Stakes,
Belmont Park, New York, 10 June 1978

THE NEWS EARLY IN 1993 THAT STEVE Cauthen would not be riding again signalled the end of one of the great Flat racing careers of the modern era. He had ridden the winners of 1,703 races in Britain in addition to 954 in his native USA and many others around the globe, but had made an impact far beyond the statistics – as a jockey of exceptional skills, with a combination of style, strength, tactical sense and exquisite judgement of pace which few of his riding rivals could approach.

Born in Kentucky on 1 May 1960, he rode his first winner on Red Pipe at River Downs on 17 May 1976, and the following year his 487 winning mounts netted over $6 million in prize money, conferring upon the teenage prodigy the soubriquet of Six Million Dollar Man. In 1978 Cauthen won the Triple Crown on Affirmed, and in spring 1979 accepted an invitation from top owner–breeder Robert Sangster to move to England.

Here the Cauthen trail continued to blaze. He won his first English race on Marquee Universal at Salisbury on 7 April 1979, and by the end of that season had added another fifty-one British winners, including the Two Thousand Guineas on Tap On Wood. In 1984 he became champion jockey – the first American to achieve the feat since Danny Maher in 1913 – and in 1985 landed four of the five English Classics: the One Thousand Guineas, Oaks and St Leger on Oh So Sharp and the Derby on Slip Anchor, thus becoming the first rider ever to have won both the Kentucky Derby and the Derby itself. Further Classic success came with Reference Point in the 1987 Derby (ridden, like Slip Anchor, from the front of the field in what was acclaimed as a masterly tactical triumph); Diminuendo in the 1988 Oaks; Snow Bride in the 1989 Oaks (awarded the race long after the event on the controversial disqualification of first-past-the-post Aliysa); and Michelozzo in the 1989 St Leger. Many other big races were won by the Cauthen magic on such stars as Old Vic, Indian Skimmer, Pebbles, In The Groove and the brilliant but enigmatic Triptych.

" Of the big races I won in Europe, a particular thrill was the 1983 Champion Stakes on Cormorant Wood, Barry Hills's wonderfully game filly who found a superb turn of foot to come from last place to first, slicing between Tolomeo and Flame Of Tara to win by a head and a short head.

But it's hard to beat winning the Derby, and my first victory, on Lord Howard de Walden's Slip Anchor in 1985, fulfilled a dream I'd had ever since watching Bill Shoemaker come so close in the race on Hawaiian Sound in 1978.

Hawaiian Sound was trained by Barry Hills and owned by Robert Sangster, and Robert had approached me about riding the colt at Epsom. Since the Derby was only three days before my Belmont Stakes date with Affirmed I thought I'd better decline, as there was always the danger of jetlag or some delay meaning that I would not be at my best for that final Triple Crown race. So I watched the Derby on television, and the sight of Bill having such a fantastic ride on Hawaiian Sound, headed almost on the line by Greville Starkey and Shirley Heights, inspired in me a great desire to ride in the race – and indeed was influential in my decision to move to Europe the following spring. Before seeing that 1978 Derby I'd never really given much thought to making such a move: afterwards I was determined to have a go.

My first ride in the Derby came in my first season in Britain, on Tap On Wood. This colt's victory in a very high-class Two Thousand Guineas (Kris was second and Young Generation third) was a very significant race in my career, as it seemed to signal the moment when the British racing public accepted me for what I was, rather than a curiosity from across the Atlantic whose arrival had been preceded by a great deal of hype.

Epsom's ups and downs, right-hand and left-hand turns, and that steep camber in the straight presented a bizarre sight to a jockey used to the sameness of the flat left-handed ovals of racetracks in the USA, but it was a challenge I always relished.

In my first Derby in 1979 Tap On Wood didn't stay, which could hardly be said of my two winners of the race, Slip Anchor and Reference Point. Over the years everyone felt the classic way to ride Epsom was the way Lester did it, laying up handy and then coming through in the straight. The point of course is that Lester was so often on a horse with an exceptional turn of foot – Sir Ivor and Nijinsky naturally come to mind – whereas if you have the right type of horse, riding in front in the Derby can be a big advantage as you're not hampered by horses falling back and interfering with you. Making the pace eliminates all the argy-bargy and the trouble you can get into coming round Tattenham Corner, and for both Slip Anchor and Reference Point making all was the ideal style of running.

Both those two must figure along with Old Vic (and of course Affirmed) among the best colts I ever rode, but I was also privileged to ride some marvellous fillies and mares. Greatest of these was certainly Oh So Sharp, winner of the fillies' Triple Crown in 1985. In many ways she reminded me of Affirmed – possessed of wonderful speed but tough as nails, very relaxed, and highly adaptable to whatever you wanted to do with her in a race.

I also had a particular affection for Pebbles (whom I partnered when in 1985 she became the first filly ever to win the Eclipse Stakes) and Indian Skimmer, who when conditions were in her favour was absolutely brilliant. And how could I forget the extraordinary Triptych, whose second Coronation Cup at Epsom in 1988 must come high in any list of the races of my life?

In the early stages she just wasn't engaged with the business in hand, letting herself get further and further adrift of the leaders. But one thing you did not do with Triptych was hustle her, so even at the top of Tattenham Hill I just had to bide my time, sit still – though I admit I was becoming just a little worried – and let her have her way until she deigned to take some interest. Sure enough, on the run down to Tattenham Corner she picked up the bit again and started to motor, and rapidly my dilemma switched from how to get her in gear to how not to let her hit the front too soon! I eased her into the lead a furlong out, at which point she put her old head in the air and decided she'd done enough, but I think she was trying to kid me, as a little urgent pushing was enough to get her home from Infamy.

'It was a real cat-and-mouse affair'

My 1978 Belmont Stakes victory on Affirmed ten years earlier may sound like an obvious choice for the race of my life, but that race still stands out more than any other in my career. There was so much riding on it.

I was eighteen years old, and already that year had partnered Affirmed to win the first two legs of the Triple Crown – the Kentucky Derby at Churchill Downs and the Preakness Stakes at Pimlico. Only ten horses had previously landed the treble, and to be on the verge of becoming a Triple Crown-winning jockey so early in my career made that Belmont Stakes the most important race I had ever taken part in.

Affirmed, trained by Laz Barrera, was a perfect horse to ride. He had great speed but you could settle him anywhere you wanted in the field and keep him handy: he'd relax and then when the moment came you could move up without setting him alight. Unlike most horses, Affirmed could be switched on and off, and he was an intelligent horse, had a great heart, and was a true battler. All in all, a wonderful horse to ride.

A special spice was given to the Triple Crown series that year by the rivalry between Affirmed and Alydar, trained by John Veitch. By the time of the Kentucky Derby, Affirmed and Alydar had already faced each other on six occasions, with the score standing at four to two in favour of Affirmed. That became five to two at Churchill Downs: Alydar was favourite but we got first run and kept on up the home stretch to win by a length and a half. In the Preakness I took up the running on Affirmed at the top of the stretch, and though Alydar mounted a tremendous challenge he was unable to pass us, the margin at the wire having shrunk to a neck. Alydar was edging closer to Affirmed with each successive leg, but could he actually get past in the Belmont?

Affirmed was odds-on favourite at 10–6 on with Alydar at 11–10 against, and only three other horses – Darby Creek Road, Judge Advocate and Noon Time Spender – took their chance against the big two.

Belmont Stakes

Belmont Park, New York, 10 June 1978 $1\frac{1}{2}$ miles

1 AFFIRMED	S. Cauthen	6–10 fav
2 Alydar	J. Velasquez	11–10
3 Darby Creek Road	A. Cordero	99–10

Also ran: Judge Advocate (4th), Noon Time Spender

5 ran   head, $13\frac{3}{4}$ lengths

Obviously Alydar, partnered by his regular jockey Jorge Velasquez, was the horse to beat, and my tactics were concentrated on how to deny him the chance to pass Affirmed. My horse could be a front-runner while his rival needed to come from behind, and in the first two legs of the Triple Crown Alydar had waited until fairly late in the race before mounting his challenge. I thought that this time his connections might attempt a change of tack, perhaps by coming at us earlier in the race and trying to wear us down, so my plan was to get Affirmed out in front and slow the pace down for as long as I could, keeping a bit up my sleeve for when Alydar came and attacked.

The Belmont Stakes starts down the home stretch, and the runners come past the Clubhouse before negotiating the first of the two turns in the race: it was important to have taken up a good position by the Clubhouse turn before heading off along the back stretch.

Alydar was drawn on my inside, but I broke well enough to be able to get clear of him and cross over to the rail, then – as we went into the first turn – started slowing the pace down as best I could. The first half mile was fairly slow and early in the back stretch I was happy enough, but with about seven furlongs to go and much sooner than he had taken issue in the previous two races, Alydar came alongside and hooked up with Affirmed. For a while it was a real cat-and-mouse affair, with myself and Jorge each biding our time, neither of us wanting to play our hand and go for everything lest that give the advantage to the other.

All along the back stretch we remained locked together, Affirmed on the inner, Alydar upsides – then, as we got to the far turn with about half a mile to go, I started gradually to quicken the pace and try to burn Alydar off. But he stuck to his guns us with amazing tenacity, and we came into the home stretch still head to head.

I had the advantage of the inside rail, but as we got to the quarter-mile pole Jorge really stoked up Alydar and went for it, and for a few seconds we were headed. Affirmed was a horse with tremendous guts, but he now found himself under the greatest pressure he'd ever known, and I was aware

Opposite:
The 1978 Belmont, with Affirmed (right) and Alydar head to head yet again.

75

that he'd have to find something very special or we'd be beaten. I'd never hit him on his left-hand side before, so I switched my stick to strike him left-handed and it seemed to give him that extra impetus. He bravely stuck his head out and clawed his way back into the lead, battling all the way to the wire to win by what was officially a head, but closer in European terms to a short head.

It had been a gruelling race – for both jockeys as well as both horses – but to have won the Triple Crown at the age of eighteen was a wonderful feeling.

Affirmed and Alydar met once more, in the Travers Stakes at Saratoga. I was sidelined through injury and the ride on Affirmed went to Laffit Pincay: they won by two lengths but were disqualified, having been judged guilty of interfering with Alydar going into the home turn.

In all Affirmed, greatest horse I rode, won twenty-two of his twenty-nine races, and now stands as a stallion in Kentucky. I go to see him whenever I can and he's still in marvellous shape: he looks like a four-year-old ready to run! **99**

Affirmed's trainer Laz Barrera once suggested that Steve Cauthen's powers in the saddle might be attributable to extraterrestrial origins: 'He came here from outer space on a flying sausage.'

If he did, bet he gave that sausage a one hell of a ride.

Peter Scudamore

Granville Again in the Smurfit Champion Hurdle, Cheltenham, 16 March 1993

TWO PAINTINGS DOMINATE THE WALLS OF THE sitting-room at Peter Scudamore's home in Gloucestershire. One is of his fall on Granville Again at the second last flight in the 1992 Champion Hurdle. The other, with pride of place above the mantelpiece, is of the same horse about to win the Champion Hurdle in 1993.

It is a large room, but would need to be cavernous were those walls to hold pictures of every winner Peter Scudamore rode. For on his retirement immediately after winning the Alpine Meadow Handicap Hurdle at Ascot on Sweet Duke on 7 April 1993 – four days after the Grand National fiasco of 'The Race That Never Was' – Scu was the most successful rider in the history of jump racing, with 1,678 winners to his credit. He was champion jump jockey a record eight times, and holds the record for wins in a single season: 221 in 1988–9.

Peter Scudamore was born on 13 June 1958, the son of Michael Scudamore, a famously tough jump jockey who won the 1957 Cheltenham Gold Cup on Linwell and the 1959 Grand National on Oxo. From an early age the young Scudamore was active in show jumping, hunter trials and hunting, and had his first ride under Rules in a Flat race at Leicester on 18 August 1975. His first ride in a point-to-point came in April the following year – he was unseated – and a few days later, at Chepstow on 19 April 1976, he made his debut under National Hunt Rules. Two years later came the first of the 1,678 winners: the twelve-year-old gelding Rolyat, trained by Toby Balding, in an amateur riders' hurdle at Devon and Exeter on 31 August 1978. Although the race did not go exactly to plan – 'Toby had told me to make all, but Rolyat whipped round at the start!' – he won unchallenged by twenty-five lengths.

Scu rode his first winner as a professional in November 1979, and notched up his first title in 1981–2, sharing the championship with John Francome: he had been well ahead when breaking his left arm in a fall at Southwell, and Francome stopped riding for the season once the scores were level. Peter Scudamore won the title outright for the first time in 1986, and in the same year rode his first Cheltenham Festival winners – Solar Cloud in the Daily Express Triumph Hurdle and Charter Party in the Ritz Club National Hunt Chase, both trained by David Nicholson, for whom Scu was stable jockey. The following year he moved to the Lambourn yard of Fred Winter, for whom he won the Champion Hurdle in 1988 on Celtic Shot.

From Winter he moved to Martin Pipe, and the partnership rewrote the record books in the 1988–9 season, Scu breaking Jonjo O'Neill's record of 149 winners in a season on the way to a sensational final tally of 221 – and a scarcely less sensational strike rate of exactly one in three. He was champion jockey again for the following three seasons, and was in second place behind Richard Dunwoody in April 1993 when surprising the racing world with news of his retirement at the age of thirty-four, to pursue fresh paths as a television pundit, journalist and assistant trainer to Nigel Twiston-Davies.

At the last: Granville Again leads from Royal Derbi (far left), with Halkopous (sheepskin noseband) and King Credo still in contention.

From such a mass of winners, how should Peter Scudamore choose the race of his life? How about, for example, the 1991 Coral Welsh National at Chepstow, when Carvill's Hill ground his rivals into the mud?

❝ There was a great deal of pressure over that race on account of Carvill's Hill having been moved to Martin Pipe from Jim Dreaper in Ireland. And there was the additional worry over whether the horse would get the trip of three and three-quarter miles. Martin is usually very bullish before a big race, but on that occasion he was concerned that the horse might go off too fast and not get home.

However it may have looked from the stands, Carvill's didn't really go faster than I'd wanted. He just found his pace and kept to it. At the end of

the first circuit, by which time he'd built up a big lead, I think he thought he'd won. He started to gurgle, so I held on to him all the way along the back second time round. The others closed on me approaching the far bend, but then he got his breath back and shot off again up the straight.

It was good to come home in that manner, but my greatest ride on Carvill's Hill was in his next race, when he won the Hennessy Cognac Gold Cup at Leopardstown. He was just fantastic that day, jumping brilliantly – apart from one mistake at the third – and winning with the proverbial head in his chest.

Winning the 1992 Scottish National for Nigel Twiston-Davies on Captain Dibble was very special. I'd schooled him the first time he ever jumped a hurdle, and rode him work before his first bumper win, so he was a horse for whom I had a great affection. It was also special as I wasn't feeling too well that day, having over-indulged in Scottish hospitality the night before. But Nigel said it was the finest race I ever rode!

My best Grand National was in 1985 on Corbiere, who had won the race two years earlier and finished third in 1984. Around Aintree he was absolutely brilliant, and his trainer Jenny Pitman really knows her horses: whenever I rode for her she would tell me precisely where I was supposed to be at each stage of the race. In that 1985 National everything went to plan – handy by second Canal Turn, kick on after Valentine's – and Corbiere was going tremendously well until the weight began to tell at the second last, when he faded a little to finish third behind Last Suspect and Young Snugfit.

Corbiere also gave me the best ride I ever had over fences, in a chase at Haydock Park in December 1986. The jumps there are big, but he found his right speed and just strode round, winning easily from Hardy Lad. He was a funny horse for a National winner – very short in front – but when you weren't rushing him he was a lovely ride.

But the race which will always stand out in my memory, and definitely the greatest training performance with which I was ever associated, was Granville Again's win in the 1993 Champion Hurdle.

As well as Granville Again, Martin Pipe had Valfinet in the Champion, and my inclination was to ride him. But Martin badgered away at me to ride the other one, and kept getting me down to Nicholashayne to ride work on Granville Again. I was not over-impressed. Granville Again tended to run away with me on the gallops, but I thought: so what? Running away on the gallops doesn't mean the horse is good enough to win the Champion Hurdle, and I thought he was too hyped up.

There were eighteen runners, including two previous winners, Kribensis and Granville Again's full brother Morley Street, but the favourite was Flown. Granville Again was second favourite although he'd not won that season: he'd run second to Morley Street at Cheltenham in November, second to Halkopous on the same course the following month, and then third behind Mighty Mogul (who had since been injured and sadly had to be put down) and Flown in the Christmas Hurdle at Kempton. He had not run since. It was asking a great deal of a horse to win a Champion Hurdle not having run since Christmas, but if any trainer could pull it off it was

Smurfit Champion Hurdle

Cheltenham, 16 March 1993   *2 miles 110 yards*

1 GRANVILLE AGAIN	P. Scudamore	13–2
2 Royal Derbi	M. Perrett	50–1
3 Halkopous	A. Maguire	9–1

Also ran: King Credo (4th), Oh So Risky, Vintage Crop, Flakey Dove, Flown, Jinxy Jack, Eyelid, Kribensis, Morley Street, Coulton, Athy Spirit, Duke of Monmouth, Valfinet, Staunch Friend, Ruling

18 ran   *1 length, 2½ lengths*

Martin Pipe, and as soon as I walked into the Cheltenham parade ring before the race I knew that he'd been right to persuade me to ride Granville Again rather than Valfinet. The horse looked so relaxed that I simply knew he was going to win, and from then on it was one of those dream races when everything goes right.

Steve Smith Eccles, who'd won the Champion Hurdle three times on See You Then, had given me great deal of advice about riding in the race, as had my father, and they both insisted that the best way to ride Cheltenham is to go wide if you're planning to come from behind. A couple of years earlier I'd ridden Granville Again in the two-mile novice hurdle at the Festival and had got stopped in my run by a horse falling in front of us. In 1992 Granville Again had been going wonderfully well coming down the hill but had tipped up at the second last. He was cantering at the time and I felt I would have won – but of course there's really no way of knowing whether he'd have beaten Royal Gait. So my plan in 1993 was to go down the middle outer – as I'd done when I'd won the race on Celtic Shot in 1988 – and keep well away from trouble.

If Granville dropped the bridle as he left the starting gate you knew he was going to go well within himself, and as the tape flew up he did just that. He went out the gate, hesitated a bit, and was clearly on good terms with himself: this was definitely his day! I always used to undo a plait of his mane once we got to the start to give me something to hold rather than hang on to his mouth, and he just cruised round, a little off the pace, in the early stages. At the top of the hill he was going so well that I was tempted to ask him to go so I could test what he had left, but decided against it: he was so relaxed, it was stupid to risk disturbing his rhythm. I didn't move on him going down the hill – and I admit I was relieved to get over the second last safely – but still arrived at the head of affairs a little bit sooner than I'd wanted, with only 50–1 outsider Royal Derbi challenging us once we'd made the turn for home.

Granville Again tended to pick up for you at a hurdle if he was going easily, but put down if under pressure, and approaching the last I asked him to go on. He put down but got over safely enough about a neck in front of Royal Derbi, then ran on stoutly up the hill to win by a length.

I was thrilled for Martin. As I said, the horse hadn't run since just after Christmas and there were plenty of people ready to carp at his form, but Martin never lost faith in the horse and had him absolutely spot-on. It was a brilliant training performance, and was in many ways the pinnacle of our association, a partnership which had meant so much to me. Critics had said that Martin could train quantity but not quality, and Granville Again's victory in the Champion Hurdle comprehensively gave the lie to that.

It was a wonderful moment. You try all the time to get that oneness with the horse, that total confidence that puts everything else out of your mind, and that day it happened.

But in any event, it's not your greatest race – it's the horse's. **"**

Tony McCoy

Viking Flagship in the Mumm Melling Chase, Aintree, 29 March 1996

IN AN ARTICLE IN THE *RACING POST* JUST BEFORE Christmas 1995, Tony McCoy, the new jump jockey sensation by then well on his way to his first championship, declared: 'I'm still waiting for that first "big" win.'

He did not have to wait long. March 1996 delivered his first Cheltenham Festival winner when Kibreet won the Grand Annual Chase, and a couple of weeks later at Aintree he rode Viking Flagship to an emphatic victory in the Mumm Melling Chase – which the same horse had won in 1995, a race described by his rider Adrian Maguire on page 35. For Tony McCoy, quality had joined quantity.

Like so many of the riders in this book, Tony McCoy comes from a racing background in Ireland – and specifically, as with Richard Dunwoody and John Reid, from Ulster: he was born in Ballymena, County Antrim, on 4 May 1974. He served his apprenticeship with Jim Bolger (where he rode work on the likes of Jet Ski Lady and St Jovite), notching up his first win with Legal Steps at Thurles on 26 March 1991. An accident when riding a Bolger two-year-old on the gallops proved the turning point of his riding life, for while he was sidelined for five and a half months his weight shot up from seven stone nine pounds to nine stone seven, and on his recovery a return to the Flat was out of the question. From now on it had to be the jumping game.

In the summer of 1994, having ridden thirteen winners in Ireland, he moved to England to join trainer Toby Balding, and by the end of the 1994–5 season had ridden seventy-four winners, breaking Adrian Maguire's record for a conditional rider. The following season – his first as a fully fledged jockey – he took the title with 175. The jump jockeys' championship had been dominated for over a decade by Peter Scudamore and Richard Dunwoody. Now the new kid on the block, completely unknown to the British racing public two years before, had arrived with a vengeance.

In an earlier *Racing Post* interview Tony McCoy had described how 'I love the thrill of riding winners, and I think about little else. The only thing I don't like about being a jockey is getting beat. If I've had a bad day at the races I definitely get down, and have a sulk.'

There was no sulking after riding Viking Flagship at Aintree.

Opposite:
**Viking Flagship and
Tony McCoy over
the final fence.**

"" Adrian Maguire had been injured earlier in the season and so couldn't partner Viking Flagship in the Queen Mother Chase, where Charlie Swan had the ride. They finished second to Klairon Davis, with Sound Man third – a great race, and a great prospect for Aintree when those three horses lined up against each other again. Coulton, who was unplaced in the Queen Mother Chase, was the fourth runner.

Charlie Swan was suspended after an incident in the Triumph Hurdle at Cheltenham and had to miss the Aintree ride on Viking Flagship, while Richard Dunwoody was committed to Sound Man. So I was delighted when David Nicholson asked me if I could ride. I'd had a few rides for the Duke earlier at the Cheltenham Festival, including Barton Bank in the Gold Cup, and I'd ridden the same horse in the Martell Cup on the opening afternoon of the big Aintree meeting – the day before the Mumm Melling Chase.

*'It was unbelievable.
I'll never have a
better ride!'*

Although we were fourth in the Gold Cup, I found Barton Bank an unbelievably difficult horse to ride: he's very good until you really get racing on him, then when you put the gun to his head he seems to forget what to do. Viking Flagship is completely the opposite: you know you're going to get a positive response, and he's a joy to ride – so gutsy and so straightforward. I'd never sat on him before getting the leg up in the paddock at Aintree, and making the acquaintance of a horse so late before a big race can be a disadvantage, but I knew perfectly well what a brilliant horse Viking Flagship was. Furthermore, he'd met all his three rivals in the Queen Mother Chase at Cheltenham, so my approach was quite relaxed. I knew he'd come out of Cheltenham well, and his performance in that thrilling 1995 Mumm Melling Chase proved that he loved the race. The ground – on the firmish side of good – was probably against Klairon Davis, and there was doubt about whether he'd get two and a half miles in this sort of company, brilliantly as he'd won over two miles at Cheltenham. Sound Man was almost certainly better over the shorter trip, and was prone to make the odd mistake – a dangerous habit for a race run as fast as this one was sure to be. It was bound to be a tough scrap, but horses do not come tougher than Viking Flagship, a really great battler and – as he'd shown with Adrian the year before – just the horse to be on in a tight finish.

Before the race he was raring to go, though at the start he was on his toes and a little reluctant to line up. The thought crossed my mind that maybe he'd seen my rather ungainly effort over the last couple of fences on his stablemate Barton Bank in the Martell Cup the day before, and was thinking: 'I'm not so sure about this McCoy chappie . . .'! But eventually he jumped off OK, and with the outsider Coulton setting a very strong pace was flat out from the start. We went a hell of a lick but I kept Coulton well in my sights, and going down the back straight second time around I stole a peep across at Richard Dunwoody on Sound Man. They were travelling very well, and with Viking Flagship not galloping that fluently I started wondering whether I'd have any response once Richard made his move: I just hoped that I could pick up and he would stop.

At the fourth last – the fence before the turn into the straight – my hopes rose when Sound Man made a bad mistake and lost a fair bit of ground.

Mumm Melling Chase

Aintree, 29 March 1996	$2\frac{1}{2}$ miles	
1 VIKING FLAGSHIP	A. P. McCoy	5–2
2 Sound Man	R. Dunwoody	6–4 fav
3 Coulton	J. A. McCarthy	8–1

Also ran: Klairon Davis (4th)

4 ran	7 lengths, $3\frac{1}{2}$ lengths	

Now Viking Flagship was travelling sweetly. Coulton could be picked off whenever I wanted, and although I let him lead us into the straight it was then time to make my move. I didn't look round to see where Sound Man or Klairon Davis were as I knew that Viking Flagship, once rousted along, would not stop. The Duke had told me that turning into the straight I'd be pretty well flat to the boards, and I wanted to be sure to stretch Sound Man and not allow him a breather to recover from that mistake. Sure enough, he never got back into the race, and Viking Flagship just set sail for home. He stood well off the second last – an open ditch – and from then on I started to enjoy myself and revel in the experience of riding a really great horse. He was well clear at the last, popped over it and ran all the way to the line to win by seven lengths from Sound Man, with Coulton third and Klairon Davis, who like Sound Man had made a bad mistake four out, last.

The Duke seemed pleased with my performance, and I was thrilled. None of the winners I'd ridden that season came anywhere near this – winning a big race on a very high-class horse, without doubt the best horse I'd ever ridden.

It was unbelievable. I'll never have a better ride! **"**

David Nicholson, never one to ration his praise of a jockey when he considers it deserved, almost pinched the title of this book when declaring after the race: 'Tony gave him the ride of a lifetime. You will never see better than that.'

Jason Weaver

Mister Baileys in the Madagans Two Thousand Guineas, Newmarket, 30 April 1994

When at the end of the 1994 Flat season the headlines were understandably hogged by Frankie Dettori's riding the winners of 233 races that year, the feat of the runner-up in the jockeys' championship went comparatively unnoticed. Yet the achievement of twenty-two-year-old Jason Weaver, rider in 1994 of 200 winners, was scarcely less sensational than that of Dettori, and as the irrepressible Italian champion soared towards the riding stratosphere, Weaver, who that season had won his first Classic when he and Mister Baileys memorably touched off Dettori and Grand Lodge in the Two Thousand Guineas, was tucked in close behind.

Jason Weaver was born on 9 February 1972 with sport in his blood, his father Eric having been a professional footballer. At school in South Wales the young Weaver's main sport was rugby union, but an early passion for riding was fuelled by his purchase of a pony – financed by the proceeds of milking cows and selling off his mother's fridge-freezer! – and honed at the British Racing School. Weaver was apprenticed to Luca Cumani's Newmarket stable – where the star turn was one Lanfranco Dettori – and rode his first winner on True Dividend at Brighton on 30 May 1990. Champion apprentice in 1993, he joined Mark Johnston at Middleham at the beginning of the 1994 season, and within weeks trainer and jockey were basking in the glow of Classic success.

66 I never sat on Mister Baileys when he was a two-year-old, but he'd had a very promising juvenile career, winning the Royal Lodge Stakes at Ascot – ridden by Frankie – on softish ground. That made us think of him more as a staying type, but at home he showed so much speed that nothing could take him on, and in the spring of 1994 we became convinced that he was a really top-class horse. I'd had the pleasure of sitting on some really good horses when I was with Luca Cumani and it's an unforgettable feeling,

sitting up there and knowing that nothing is capable of going past you. Mister Baileys gave me very much the same sort of feel: you'd say, 'Go on a stride, go on a stride' and he would – he'd just keep finding more.

Until quite close to the race it was still very much up in the air whether I would ride him in the Guineas. Dean McKeown had ridden him on most of his two-year-old outings but had gone to Hong Kong, Frankie was booked for Grand Lodge, and all the other jockeys who'd been approached had turned him down, presumably because they thought he just wasn't good enough. The punters seemed to share that view, as not long before the race Mister Baileys was still a 33–1 chance, but when it was confirmed that I'd be on him – my first ride in a Classic – I was over the moon.

Mister Baileys went to the Guineas without a previous race as a three-year-old, but we'd put him through his paces well enough at home and weren't bothered that he'd fail on account of being less than one hundred per cent fit. What concerned us more was the possibility that he'd be beaten by speedier types on the day, and it was certainly a pretty high-class Guineas field. King's Theatre, who had won the Craven Stakes, was favourite, with Unblest and Colonel Collins next in the betting; Mister Baileys started at 16–1, the same price as Grand Lodge, who had won the Dewhurst Stakes as a two-year-old but had been only sixth in the Craven on his reappearance at three.

There was a lot of rubbish talked about the draw before the 1994 Guineas, with people saying that after the course had been watered earlier in the week

'My fellow stuck his nose out where it mattered': Jason Weaver and Mister Baileys (right) pip Frankie Dettori and Grand Lodge.

the ground towards the far side of the Rowley Mile was significantly faster than up the stands side. Mister Baileys was drawn on the far side at twenty-one of the twenty-three runners, and Grand Lodge at twenty-two, but as far as I was concerned the draw meant nothing: the best horse on the day would win, and I knew that my fellow would run a big race. Although it was my first Classic I wasn't nervous, as I knew that Mister Baileys was spot-on and it was simply a pleasure to be on board such a horse.

Since we had no doubts about his stamina, the key was to keep him handy and not ask him for any sudden burst of acceleration, and the race gave me no problems at all. We jumped smartly out of the stalls and settled down into a good pace, always travelling well. Three furlongs out I looked across to the main bunch of runners, who were beginning to close up and make their moves. I decided to let Mister Baileys go. Away he went into the lead, and the rest is history. About a quarter of a mile out we were joined by Grand Lodge and Frankie, and had a tremendous battle all the way to the line. Grand Lodge nearly headed me but couldn't quite manage it, as my fellow stuck his nose out where it mattered and held on by a short head. It looked very close, but I knew we'd won.

It was a fantastic feeling, winning my first Classic after such a battle with Frankie. He and I had become great mates when we were together at Luca Cumani's, and as we eased down and pulled up he slapped me on the back: 'Well done, matey – you've won it!' We had – and in the fastest time ever clocked for the Two Thousand Guineas, beating the record set by Zafonic the year before.

Going back to the winner's enclosure was just a blur, and when I got home that evening there were what seemed like hundreds of messages of congratulation on my answering machine, followed by piles of letters throughout the following week. It was just wonderful.

Mister Baileys then went on to the Dante Stakes at York, but could only finish third behind Erhaab and Weigh Anchor, a defeat widely put down to lack of stamina. We weren't convinced that he didn't stay, however, and it was decided not only that he would take his chance in the Derby, but that I'd ride him on the assumption that he would get the trip: perhaps, we thought, he didn't like being held up at York, and it would be better to let him go on.

At Epsom he gave me the most fantastic ride: I've never ridden a horse who tried so hard and gave so much. After about half a mile he took up the running, and going down the hill into Tattenham Corner I let him have another half inch of rein and he responded electrically, going into a six-length lead as we reached the straight – though at the time I didn't know how far ahead we were. But he couldn't get home and inside the final quarter of a mile I could hear the pack closing on me. His stride began to shorten, and just over a furlong out he was passed by Colonel Collins and King's Theatre, and then by Willie Carson staging his whirlwind finish on Erhaab. But he dug deep and ran hard to the line to finish fourth – a great performance. Afterwards he was so exhausted he could hardly stand up, and I have to say that the race left its mark on him.

'Mister Baileys had a heart bigger than any horse I've had the pleasure to sit on'

Madagans Two Thousand Guineas

Newmarket, 30 April 1994 — *1 mile*

1	MISTER BAILEYS	J. Weaver	16–1
2	Grand Lodge	L. Dettori	16–1
3	Colonel Collins	J. Reid	13–2

Also ran: State Performer (4th), Distant View, Star Selection, River Deep, Just Happy, Rafferty's Rules, Canaska Dancer, Cotteir Chief, Dumaani, King's Theatre, Torch Rouge, Unblest, Golden Nashwan, Indhar, Redoubtable, Signe Divin, Piccolo, Suplizi, Cool Jazz, Crazy Paving

23 ran *short head, 3 lengths*

Some people said I'd gone for home too soon on a doubtful stayer and should have held him up, but I disagree – and I'd ride the same race again. He was a difficult horse to settle, would run very keen, and in any case we hadn't set a blistering pace. It's often the case in the Derby that a runner who truly stays a mile and a quarter will get home over the extra two furlongs, and we thought he'd stay. Why disappoint the horse by holding him up?

Mister Baileys had a heart bigger than any horse I've had the pleasure to sit on. **"**

Norman Williamson

Master Oats in the Tote Cheltenham Gold Cup, Cheltenham, 16 March 1995

A JUMP JOCKEY'S LIFE IS ONE OF UPS AND downs. That most obvious of racing clichés has rarely been more spectacularly illustrated than by the contrast for Norman Williamson between the Cheltenham National Hunt Festivals of 1995 and 1996.

At the 1995 staging of jump racing's greatest annual jamboree Williamson could do no wrong. Winning the Ritz Club Trophy for most successful rider of the meeting, he scaled heights few jockeys have ever reached when landing the Champion Hurdle on Alderbrook and the Gold Cup on Master Oats, both for trainer Kim Bailey, thus becoming the first rider to land this rare double since Fred Winter on Eborneezer and Saffron Tartan in 1961.

A year on, Williamson's riding life had

turned very sour. In April 1995 he suffered two sprained ankles and a badly bruised thigh in a schooling accident; three months later a fall in a race at Stratford left him with a dislocated right shoulder and fractured left wrist; he returned to action but was sidelined again when breaking his right leg in a fall at Sedgefield in October. This introduced a question mark over his chances of going for the repeat Cheltenham double on Alderbrook and Master Oats, but he was back race-riding on 8 February 1996 – only to dislocate his right shoulder again in a fall in the Tote Gold Trophy at Newbury just two days later. On 28 February, by which time Alderbrook had made an impressive return to hurdling and looked a good thing for the 1996 Champion Hurdle, and Master Oats was a still a leading Gold Cup contender, Williamson was cleared by a specialist for another return to the saddle, then on 1 March injured his shoulder yet again during a schooling session, and was ruled out for the rest of the season. So it goes . . .

Born in Mallow, County Cork on 16 January 1969, Norman Williamson served his apprenticeship as an amateur rider for Dermot Weld, riding his first winner, Jack And Jill, at Clonmel on 19 May 1988. After moving to England in 1989 he rode as stable jockey for John Edwards, for whom he won big races on such good horses as Monsieur Le Cure and 1990 Mackeson Gold Cup winner Multum In Parvo. In 1993 he teamed up with Kim Bailey, an association which soon brought great rewards, and their second season together climaxed in that heady Cheltenham Festival double, the second leg of which provided Norman Williamson with his greatest moment – to date.

❝ The 1995 Cheltenham Gold Cup on Master Oats has to be my greatest race, with Alderbrook's Champion Hurdle a very close second – the difference between them being that the Champion, both in the planning and in the actual race, was much more straightforward than the Gold Cup.

I first rode Master Oats in a handicap chase at Uttoxeter in November 1993, on his return from a long lay-off. At that stage neither Kim Bailey nor I had any idea what a talent we had in our care, and I found him a difficult horse to get to know – oddly, in fact, the better he got, the more difficult he was to know. Through the middle of the 1993–4 season he improved hugely, turning in an amazing performance to win the Greenall Whitley Chase, transferred from Haydock to Kempton Park, by fifteen lengths, on the bridle. Admittedly he had a light weight, but it was only from that point that we had a real idea of how good he was – and we realised that he would only be ever seen at his best on soft ground.

Moorcroft Boy, third in the Greenall, went on to run third to Miinnehoma in the Grand National, so on form my fellow should have won the National by ten lengths. But Master Oats fell at the thirteenth in the 1994 National, and that was that.

The following season he opened his account on his seasonal debut in the Rehearsal Chase at Chepstow, beating 1992 National winner Party Politics. He won that day by just keeping going rather than showing much of a turn of foot, but on New Year's Eve in the Welsh National – run at Newbury as Chepstow was unraceable – he quickened up early in the straight, jumped the last three fences in his stride and kept accelerating all the way up the run-in.

Some people were getting very excited about Master Oats but we felt we were still learning about him, and the key was clearly the ground: in very soft conditions he could pick up and increase the pace, whereas on a faster surface the others could quicken and he couldn't. It was only after Newbury that Kim Bailey and I started to take him seriously as a Gold Cup proposition. As a prep race he went to Cheltenham for the Pillar Chase at the end of January, and on soft going won very easily from Dubacilla and Barton Bank.

The 1995 Gold Cup was the first occasion on which Master Oats had come up against a big field of top-class chasers on level terms. We were stepping into unknown territory – but when the ground on the day came up soft I thought he was a certainty, and the market reflected his obvious credentials: he started favourite at 100–30, with Jodami, Barton Bank and Miinnehoma next in the betting.

By Gold Cup afternoon, the third day of the meeting – and the final Festival day, though that year there was an extra non-Festival fixture at Cheltenham on the Friday – I was already on a high. Alderbrook's victory in the Champion Hurdle on the Tuesday was my first ever winner at this great meeting, and its sweet taste was made even sweeter by the contrast with my experience the previous year, when through suspension I'd missed

Opposite:
After the Gold Cup –
Norman Williamson
jumping for joy.

92

what would have been a winning Champion Hurdle ride on Flakey Dove. In 1995 the Festival had gone like a dream. Alderbrook on the Tuesday, Putty Road and Kadi on the Wednesday – three victories on the first two days, and I was flying.

In the race itself my plan was to travel easily, just off the pace, for the first circuit and put Master Oats into contention halfway round the second; but Merry Gale and Monsieur Le Cure set a hell of a pace, and with Jodami, Miinnehoma and Flashing Steel all very close it was not as easy to settle as I'd hoped. He jumped round most of the first circuit well, but at the fence at the bottom of the hill made an almighty blunder, and when I look at the photographs of it now I just don't know how he stood up. On the approach we were four or five lengths behind Graham Bradley on the leader Merry Gale, with plenty of space and time for Master Oats to get a proper look at it, but he just seemed to walk straight through it. He did this occasionally, and, being such a big, well-built horse, usually got away with it; this time his nose was on the floor, and it was probably only luck which kept me in the saddle.

"'Holy F*!
You're running
away!'"**

I'm sure that mistake took more out of me than him. He'd jumped very well indeed at Newbury and in his last race at Cheltenham, and to find that he could miss one out sent my confidence into a nose-dive. Had it been a run-of-the-mill chase I might well have called it a day after such a mistake, but this was the Gold Cup and I had to rebuild his rhythm and my confidence: after all, we were still standing, still in one piece and still in with a chance. I gave him a smack to waken him up for the next fence, and he responded by jumping really well.

As we set out on the second circuit the pace hotted up and we were starting to get competitive, and disaster had one more go at stopping him. Going to the first fence on the second circuit Master Oats was on the inner, and in danger of getting hemmed in as the pace quickened. I tried to manoeuvre him out to get more room and give him a better opportunity to see the fence, but I couldn't move. About ten strides off the fence I was right on the heels of the horse in front, with two on my outside and one on my inner. There was no room for changing course and it was too late to do anything about it, so I just prayed that Master Oats would be able to see the fence and jump it. He's not the brightest of horses, not the sort to think ahead and avoid trouble, and as usual he was relying on me to put him right. He walloped the birch, somehow managed to keep his feet, but had lost his position so badly that I felt I couldn't possibly win from there. He wasn't jumping well, he wasn't even travelling smoothly: why persist? But the Gold Cup is the Gold Cup . . .

This was a do-or-die moment. I decided to switch him wide and try to get up among the leaders. Normally I wouldn't have acted so soon, but would have tried to sit quiet for another two fences and maybe wait until the top of the hill before making my move. But this wasn't normal. I was desperate – things were going so badly that I just had to do something to get Master Oats back into his rhythm. He jumped the water and the fence after that well, and then things started to happen around us. Flashing Steel

Tote Cheltenham Gold Cup

Cheltenham, 16 March 1995   *3 miles 2½ furlongs*

1 MASTER OATS	N. Williamson	100–30 fav
2 Dubacilla	D. Gallagher	20–1
3 Miinnehoma	R. Dunwoody	9–1

Also ran: Merry Gale (4th), Young Hustler, Monsieur Le Cure, Beech Road, Jodami, Commercial Artist, Barton Bank, Flashing Steel, Algan, Nuaffe, Val d'Alene, Deep Bramble

15 ran   *15 lengths, 15 lengths*

fell, Monsieur Le Cure nearly came down, and Barton Bank fell on the uphill stretch – I think he was running on empty by then. From being in despair a few moments earlier, I was now, at the top of the hill with three fences to go and only Merry Gale an apparent danger, starting to get very confident. The further we went the stronger Master Oats felt under me, and most of the others were becoming very tired. Master Oats and Merry Gale were making the best of their way home, and I was just hoping that there was nothing behind us going well enough to raise a challenge.

As we turned down the hill Graham Bradley took a peep behind and announced – in characteristic Brad fashion – 'Holy F***! You're running away! We're twenty-five lengths clear!' I knew then that if Master Oats jumped the last three fences – that year there was only one in the finishing straight – we would win the Gold Cup. As we skipped over the third last Master Oats was absolutely hacking, and although Merry Gale was still on terms it was really a matter of going on whenever I wanted.

Round the last bend we set sail for home, but I never at any stage looked back so was not aware that Dubacilla was making late progress to move into second. Nothing was going to get anywhere near me – a great feeling! As we came to the last I was well aware of the roar of the crowd, but it did not bother Master Oats in the slightest. He jumped the last really well and galloped all the way to the line: a horse like that is never going to stop.

To have landed the Gold Cup having come so close to disaster, and to have won the race after having lifted the Champion Hurdle at the same meeting, was a fantastic thrill – the greatest moment of my riding life.

Kim Bailey and I had a bit of a night out that evening – nothing too serious, as we were racing again the next day – and then thoughts turned to running Master Oats in the Grand National, not only to eradicate the unfortunate memory of the previous year but to put him up there with Golden Miller as a winner of the Gold Cup and Grand National in the same year. Even with top weight he clearly had a major chance, and in the event ran what was probably the race of *his* life, though the ground was not soft enough for him. As in the Gold Cup he switched suddenly from not travelling at all well to going very smoothly, and he was in contention right up to the final fence; but unsurprisingly he faded on the run-in to come seventh behind Royal Athlete. It was a wonderful effort. **"**

Master Oats was not able to defend his Gold Cup crown in 1996, succumbing to a leg injury in the run-up to the race and being retired for the season. Alderbrook, on the other hand, did run in the Champion Hurdle: ridden by Richard Dunwoody, he was outgunned up the run-in by Graham Bradley and Collier Bay and finished second, beaten two and a half lengths.

So at least Norman Williamson, spending the 1996 Cheltenham Festival as a paddock pundit for Channel Four Racing, did not have to stand on the sidelines as other riders won the big races on what were normally his rides – for a jump jockey a pain that aches far more than any broken leg or dislocated shoulder.

John Reid

THE CAREER OF JOHN REID ILLUSTRATES THE old adage that good horses make good jockeys – that it takes association with one good horse, victory in one very big race, to propel a rider towards the upper reaches of the sport. In Reid's case that first good horse was Ile de Bourbon, on whom he won the King George VI and Queen Elizabeth Diamond Stakes in July 1978, just over five years after his first winner. His partnership with that fine horse drew his skills to the attention of the leading trainers, and in no time he was right up there in the top bracket, a stylish, effective, articulate and highly popular rider whose career has deservedly gone from strength to strength.

John Reid was born in County Down on 6 August 1955, and served his apprenticeship at Didcot with Verly Bewicke – trainer of his first winner, Eyry in the Cucumber Maiden Stakes at Goodwood on 16 May 1973. In 1978 he joined Fulke Johnson Houghton, and stayed with the stable until 1983, by which time he had landed his first English Classic on 33–1 outsider On The House, trained by Harry Wragg, in the 1982 One Thousand Guineas. On The House – and Reid – went on to land the Sussex Stakes at Goodwood the same season.

In June 1987 he won the Irish Derby on Sir Harry Lewis, who earlier the same month had given him his best ride – to that date – in the Epsom Derby, finishing fourth behind Reference Point; and his talents were appreciated on a wider international stage in October 1988 when he drove the Italian-trained Tony Bin to a storming victory over Mtoto in the Prix de l'Arc de Triomphe. That same year he took a prestigious retainer with the doyen of Irish trainers Vincent O'Brien, which lasted until 1990, but his injury following a fall from Whippet before the start of the Prix de l'Abbaye at Longchamp on Arc day 1990 deprived him of the ride on O'Brien's Royal Academy in the Breeders' Cup Mile at Belmont Park that year – a spare ride famously picked up by a fifty-four-year-old jockey making a come-back from retirement, and described by that rider on pages 5–6.

Longchamp two years before the Whippet injury had much happier memories for John Reid.

❝ In 1988 I was going through a somewhat turbulent time in my career. I had the plum job as jockey for Vincent O'Brien, but that season I had twice gone against my better judgement to ride one O'Brien runner in an Irish Classic rather than another I'd originally thought I should ride, only to suffer the experience of seeing the other one win. I'd ridden Caerwent rather than Prince of Birds in the Irish Two Thousand Guineas: Prince of Birds, ridden by Declan Gillespie, beat us a neck. Later in the season I rode Kris Kringle rather than Dark Lomond in the Irish St Leger: Dark Lomond won, Kris Kringle was unplaced.

A few days before that race I'd been phoned from Italy and asked if I could ride Tony Bin in his Arc prep race in Milan the day after the Irish Leger – and if so, could I also ride him in the Arc? I was aware that Tony Bin was a pretty useful horse, who had finished second to Trempolino in the Arc the year before, and I knew he'd be a great ride at Longchamp, so I accepted promptly.

But travelling back from Ireland on the Saturday evening after the Irish Leger, having got off Dark Lomond, I was in despair. Having arrived at Heathrow I phoned my wife Joy to say that I was in such a bad mood that I'd book into a hotel near the airport and fly straight out to Milan for the ride on Tony Bin. In the hotel I downed about four gin and tonics and went to bed not a happy man at all.

I felt a great deal better the following day after winning on Tony Bin, who gave me a fantastic feel – he won doing handsprings – and returned home convinced that I had got myself an Arc ride with a real chance. About two hours after I got home the phone rang. It was Vincent O'Brien's office at Ballydoyle, telling me that Dark Lomond was going to run in the Arc, and as I was the retained jockey I would naturally be riding her. Despair again: how could I pass up the opportunity to ride Tony Bin in favour of Dark Lomond, who was a good filly but essentially a stayer, with little chance of being speedy enough for the Arc? I pleaded to be let off and Vincent agreed, providing he could find a decent jockey for his filly, and once Freddie Head was booked I was able to keep the ride on Tony Bin.

I'm glad I did. He was a funny horse: if you went into his box he'd try to bite a piece out of you, but he had tremendous spirit and masses of ability. I'd ridden in the Arc before – Ile de Bourbon, unplaced in 1979, was my first ride in the race – and during the run-up to the 1988 race had read an article by Yves Saint-Martin in which he said an Arc jockey should never make a move until you get out of the 'false straight', the stretch before the finishing straight proper.

The race went very well. I jumped Tony Bin out of the stalls and had him in a nice position climbing to the top of the hill. We then encountered a bit of trouble coming down the hill as Derby winner Kahyasi got squeezed badly in front of us, forcing us to check our stride and go round him. Then just as I was moving out Cash Asmussen on Village Star came up on our outside. I did not want to take my chance up the inner, where the risk of getting chopped off was always present, so was intending to go round the outside. But Cash did not want me to push him out as I made my move, and shouted at me, 'Not yet, Johnny, don't go yet!' – not for my benefit, but his! He held me there until we reached the straight proper, and then I set sail for home. Perhaps Tony Bin got to the front a little bit sooner than I'd intended, and that last furlong felt a very long one. Mtoto came out of the pack and was catching us hand over fist, but Tony Bin stuck to his guns wonderfully well, and we held on by a neck.

The reception afterwards was unbelievable, with people running out on to the track, lying down and thanking the Lord, and mobbing the horse – who did not much appreciate that level of attention. When we got back to the paddock to unsaddle I could hardly dismount, such was the crush. We ended up having dinner at the Ritz. The next day I rode at Bath.

However wonderful it was when it happened, winning the Arc had somehow never been a particular ambition of mine: it had always seemed one of those races that was out of reach, and until Tony Bin's year I'd never really seen myself winning it. The Derby, on the other hand, was the Derby . . .

Since I'd been a kid I'd dreamed about winning the Derby, but before 1992 I'd never gone into the race with what I felt was a realistic chance. I'd ridden in the race seven times, with the fourth on Sir Harry Lewis in 1987 my best placing, and this was quite enough experience to show what a difficult race it is. A mile and half at Epsom is completely unlike any other trip, with its right- and then left-hand turns, uphill and downhill, and that trappy camber up the straight. The qualities a Derby horse most needs are speed and balance, and I knew that my ride in 1992 had those in abundance.

Dr Devious, trained by Peter Chapple-Hyam, had had a busy time as a two-year-old, winning four of his six races – notably the Dewhurst Stakes, top two-year-old race of the season – and finishing runner-up in the others. He had been sold by Robert Sangster to Luciano Gaucci (the Gauccis had owned Tony Bin), and before the start of his three-year-old career had been sold again, being bought by the American businesswoman Jenny Craig as a sixtieth birthday present for her husband Sidney.

Peter Chapple-Hyam had asked me to ride for him the previous year – his first as a trainer – but I'd declined due to other commitments, and my Derby ride on Dr Devious was my first for the stable. Dr Devious had run in the Kentucky Derby and finished seventh (one place ahead of Arazi), but had recovered extraordinarily well from his exertions and was being trained for Epsom. It was a couple of weeks before the race that my agent called and told me that the Derby ride was going spare. Did I want to ride him? Too right I did!

I went to Manton to sit on the horse for the first time, and he gave me a hell of a feel. He was not big, but was very compact and had a nice easy action, and felt exceptionally well balanced around the bends – simply the ideal type of horse for Epsom, an impression reinforced by a superb final piece of work at home. The next time I sat on him was at the racecourse on the day before the Derby, when we went for a little spin down the hill: Lester Piggott was on Two Thousand Guineas winner Rodrigo De Triano in the big race, and after he'd seen Dr Devious come down the hill so well he said to me: 'I wouldn't mind riding your one instead!'

'Through the last furlong I was saying to myself, "Where's the line? Where's the line?"'

The Derby is not a race I would greatly look forward to when riding a no-hoper, but on the morning of Derby Day 1992 I woke up full of confidence. I was not riding work that morning, so had the luxury of Joy bringing me tea and newspapers in bed. I said to her: 'I really think I'm going to win the Derby today.'

I'd discussed the race often enough with Peter Chapple-Hyam, but on the day he left the tactics to me. Assuming you have the right sort of horse under you – a very large assumption for most jockeys most years! – the ideal way to ride the Derby is to have enough speed to get up into the first half dozen soon after the start, then keep that position. If you're too far back you can get into trouble when the bunching and scrimmaging begins at the top of the hill: with everybody trying to get a position and hold it, the Derby is usually a very rough race. You have to judge how quick they're going, how much you're going to use your horse to hold a position, without ending up with nothing left for the finish. The plan was to reach that vital position and then get the horse to relax – easier said than done with Dr Devious, a horse who liked racing and was very keen: he had to have that enthusiasm channelled to make best use of it.

He was quite unbothered by the preliminaries and once in the stalls he stood there very quietly. At the off he hit the gate very fast, and in the first part of the race he was running very free. When after negotiating the first – right-handed – turn we crossed over to the inside rail I found myself in about third position, with the horse still taking a hold and running very freely. My most urgent need was to get him to settle: if he didn't relax, he wouldn't win. So I spoke to him: 'Whoa, whoa . . . come back, come back,' but he wouldn't calm down, and for another furlong he pulled me along as I tried to persuade him to settle by trying to get him back, then leaving him, then trying to get him back, then leaving him . . .

Eventually, after the best part of half a mile, he dropped the bit: thank God for that! From then on the race went like a dream. I had a nice position, two or three off the fence, with horses in front of me, and all the way down to Tattenham Corner I was freewheeling: by now he was no longer pulling, just going well within himself. There had been a slight question mark over his stamina (his sire was the sprinter Ahonoora) but my view was that he would stay. In any case, either he would or he wouldn't, and I was not inclined to ride a fancy race and come very late – better to work on the assumption that he would stay.

Coming round Tattenham Corner he was third behind Twist And Turn and Great Palm. Once we were in the straight I eased him out and started making up ground on the leaders, going for one long run without doing anything too sudden, and taking the lead inside the final two furlongs. He galloped all the way to the line, and it was an unbelievable feeling when I could see the winning post. Although the minor placings were being sorted out behind us – St Jovite beat Silver Wisp a short head for second – nothing challenged, and as we passed the post I did something I'd never done in my life before: took one hand off the reins and punched the air. It was such a great feeling: I'd won the Derby and I couldn't believe it. Through the last furlong I was saying to myself, 'Where's the line? Where's the line?', but as we went over it I knew that there would be no questioning the result: no photo-finish, no stewards' enquiry, just a clean-cut win. Past the post – YES! MADE IT!!

I can't remember too many details about the immediate post-race bedlam. On the evening of the race Joy and I went out with Jane and Peter Chapple-Hyam – who had done such a superb job on the horse in only his second season as a trainer – to a Chinese restaurant in Marlborough, and had a celebration party at home the following Sunday.

The sheer euphoria of winning the Derby lasted five or six days, but there were more lasting effects. For the first time my children – especially my son Joe, who was seven – realised what it meant for their father to be a jockey: Joe had been asked about it at school, which got him interested in what his father did, and now he wanted to talk to me about it all!

When Dr Devious met St Jovite again in the Irish Derby at The Curragh he was starting to get sick, and ran very flat: we were beaten twelve lengths into second place. He was coming back from that illness when fourth behind

'Past the post – YES! MADE IT!!'

Ever Ready Derby

Epsom, 3 June 1992		$1\frac{1}{2}$ miles	
1 DR DEVIOUS	J. Reid		8–1
2 St Jovite	C. Roche		14–1
3 Silver Wisp	Paul Eddery		11–1

Also ran: Muhtarram (4th), Twist And Turn, Alflora, Alnasr Alwasheek, Great Palm, Rodrigo De Triano, Thourious, Rainbow Corner, Well Saddled, Assessor, Paradise Navy, Lobilio, Pollen Count, Ninja Dancer, Young Freeman

18 ran	*2 lengths, short head*

Rodrigo De Triano in the Juddmonte International Stakes at York in August, and was reaching his peak again when he went to Leopardstown for his pre-Arc race, meeting St Jovite and the good filly Kooyonga in the Irish Champion Stakes.

In the Irish Derby I had suffered a fair bit of trouble. St Jovite's trainer Jim Bolger had two other horses in the race, and they'd given us some hassle, which I'd not been best pleased about. Likewise in the Irish Champion Stakes there was another Bolger runner in the shape of Magic Carr, who couldn't possibly win but might cause me problems. Peter and I discussed the race, and decided that in the circumstances the best course would be to drop Dr Devious out and avoid taking on Magic Carr. On the morning of the race I was walking the track when I met St Jovite's rider Christy Roche, who was of the firm opinion that the ground on the inside was terrible: we'd better go wide, he said. I agreed, though I couldn't see much wrong with the ground on the inner.

There was plenty of pace in the race but Dr Devious was running well within himself in the early stages. Coming out of the back straight Magic Carr dropped back to come upsides me, at which point I kicked on. At the home turn Christy, true to his word, went wide and took a lead of about a length and half. I went up the inside and got to him, he drifted back in a little, and from then on – all the way up the straight – it was nip and tuck. St Jovite seemed to be getting the better of us but Dr Devious was a tremendous battler and just wouldn't give in, and we were head to head for what felt like an age. Just before the line it looked as if we'd be narrowly beaten, but my fellow fought back once more and as we passed the post I simply didn't know whether I'd won or not. Leopardstown has a very wide finishing line, and in a finish that tight it was impossible to judge. But the photo gave it to us by a short head. It had been a truly great race, but it probably flattened both horses for the Arc: Dr Devious was sixth at Longchamp, just behind St Jovite in fourth. Dr Devious finished one place ahead of Arc winner Subotica when fourth in the Breeders' Cup Turf at Gulfstream Park, Florida, and ended his long, hard season by running tenth in the Japan Cup: I did not ride him that day, the Craigs having decided to put up American jockey Chris McCarron.

Dr Devious was a wonderfully tough and genuine performer – and he certainly gave me the race of my life. 🟆🟆

Josh Gifford

Major Rose in the Schweppes Gold Trophy, Newbury, 17 February 1968

JOSHUA THOMAS GIFFORD RODE 642 WINNERS over jumps in a National Hunt career which spanned a decade from 1959 to 1969 and saw him champion jockey four times – 1962–3, 1963–4, 1966–7 (with the then record total of 122 winners) and 1967–8 – before retiring to begin a new and equally successful life as a trainer. Taking over the Findon yard of his old guv'nor Ryan Price, for whom he had won many big races, Gifford the trainer has been responsible for such fine horses as Kybo, Deep Sensation, Brief Gale and Bradbury Star – and, most famously, Aldaniti. That horse's victory in the 1981 Grand National partnered by Bob Champion, whose recovery from cancer had been bolstered by Gifford's assurance that his job as stable jockey was his however long it took him to get well, is the stuff of racing legend.

Born on 3 August 1941, Josh Gifford was apprenticed to Cliff Beechener and then to Fred Armstrong. He rode fifty-one winners on the Flat – including Curry in the 1957 Chester Cup – before increasing weight turned his attention to the National Hunt code. He joined Ryan Price, rode his first jumping winner in 1959 (Kingmaker in a novices' hurdle at Wincanton on 17 December), and took over as stable jockey on the retirement of Fred Winter in 1964. For Price he won the Schweppes Gold Trophy four times, and other big-race triumphs included the Triumph Hurdle on Beaver II in 1962, the Welsh Grand National on Forty Secrets in 1962, the Mackeson Gold Cup on Charlie Worcester in 1967, and the Whitbread Gold Cup on Larbawn in 1969.

Unusually among the contributors to this book – but not uniquely – he chooses as the race of his life a contest which he did not win.

" There's no doubt that the race which loomed largest in my riding life – in general terms – was the Schweppes Gold Trophy (the precursor of what is now the Tote Gold Trophy at Newbury). It was always a very lucky race for me: I won four of the first five runnings on horses trained by Ryan Price, and in the sixth running, though beaten, had what I've long thought of as the best race I ever rode.

The first Schweppes was run not at Newbury but at Liverpool, the day before the 1963 Grand National. I rode Rosyth, a horse whose apparent chance was illustrated not only by his starting price of 20–1, but also by the fact that neither his owner nor the old man – Ryan Price – bothered to travel up for the race. I tended to agree with them that flogging up there was a bit of a waste of time as the horse had little recent form to commend him, but stable jockey Fred Winter did not want to ride him at ten stone so I was packed off on the overnight train, with instructions from the old man that I was to go to the Adelphi Hotel and book into the room reserved in his name to have a kip before going off to the racecourse. When I got to the Adelphi they wouldn't let me have his room so I had to snatch a couple of hours' sleep on a couch while the cleaning ladies did their work all around me: not the ideal preparation for a big race.

That initial running was worth £7,825 2s 6d to the winner, a massive amount for a handicap hurdle in those days, and attracted a huge field of forty-one runners. There were no safety limits back then and we had to make two lines at the starting gate, which gave rise to a good deal of joking about 'fancied ones in the front row, others behind'. But a field of that size belting around the tight Liverpool hurdle circuit was no joke, particularly for Stan Mellor, who at the second flight took a terrible fall from Eastern Harvest which left him badly injured. It was a mad scramble and many of the fancied horses got knocked about, while I had all the luck in running and won by a length from Royal Jenny.

It was clearly daft to run that sort of race at Liverpool, and the following year it was moved to Newbury, a much more spacious and sensible track. Rosyth had run very disappointingly in the run-up to a repeat Schweppes, but he was an entire horse, not a gelding, and used to come right in the spring, when his form tended to improve dramatically. The change was extraordinary: early on in the season he'd be quite useless, then he'd blossom.

When we realised early in 1964 that he was starting to improve, the old man started to think that if he got ten stone in the Schweppes it was worth having another go: 'If he comes back to himself like he did last year we'll have a crack at winning that bloody race again.' And so Rosyth was laid out for the Schweppes.

Before Rosyth's prep race at Sandown Park in January, the old man's view was that although the horse was coming back to himself he wasn't right just yet. 'He's a colt, don't be hard on him,' he told me, adding that whatever happened I had to weigh out at his allotted weight of ten stone. I managed to pass the scales at that mark, but after a cup of tea and a sandwich and making one or two little adjustments to my gear ended up carrying ten three or ten four. In the circumstances I didn't particularly want to weigh in, so in the race I dropped my hands close home and managed to avoid coming fourth in order to duck a dispute with the clerk of the scales: Rosyth finished sixth, nine lengths behind the winner Salmon Spray.

'I timed my challenge perfectly and did everything right – bar winning!'

Obviously getting beaten in that race with ten stone did little to advertise Rosyth's chance in the Schweppes, and he was given ten two. The day before the race Johnny Haine told me that his ride Salmon Spray was a certainty, and that Rosyth's win the previous year had been a fluke: I advised him not to look round jumping the last or he might get a shock. In the event I managed to have a little chat with Johnny as Rosyth sailed past Salmon Spray at the second last, and my horse won well: too well for the liking of the Jockey Club, who thought that beating Salmon Spray by two lengths on only four pounds better terms than when he had beaten us at Sandown smelled sufficiently for the old man to lose his licence until the end of the season and for me to be suspended for six weeks.

Rosyth was a smashing little horse when right, useless when wrong. He used to break blood vessels, and when he did so the old man would take him out and gallop him the very next day. You can't do that with most horses, but it worked with him. A couple of days before his second Schweppes we took him for a gallop at Fontwell Park and he burst. The old man's reaction was: 'That's good – that'll put him just right!' And as usual, he wasn't wrong.

Had I been able to ride Rosyth – then in the care of Tom Masson – in the 1965 race we might well have won for the third year running, as his rider that day Johnny Gilbert did not know him well and they were only just beaten by David Nicholson on Elan.

In 1966 I won my third Schweppes on Le Vermontois, only a novice but a very good horse whose career was blighted by hock trouble. Ryan Price had an uncanny knack of being able to get a horse right at the right time, and Le Vermontois was a classic case: at Newbury he kicked the last flight of hurdles out of the ground but still won by half the track.

Then in 1967 there was Hill House. On a very foggy day in November 1966 I rode him in the Mackeson Hurdle at Cheltenham. We thought he would win, and I was in third or fourth place on the inside going down the back side when, as so often happens at Cheltenham, the horses in front of us bunched up and we were absolutely mangled and knocked back to last place. That obliterated our chance, but I got him running again and he ran past most of the field to finish fourth. I came back to the old man and reported:

'This is a cert for the Schweppes. I got mangled!'

'Mangled? Say no more, Josha' – he only called me Josha when I was in his good books, so that wasn't very often – 'Say no more,' and the plan was laid.

Shortly after that race I went to the stables at Findon to ride out and noticed that Hill House was not in his box: he'd been sent back to his owner. I asked why.

'I don't want to see that horse for six weeks,' said Ryan Price: 'He'll win the Schweppes. Sent him home – do him the world of good. He's a temperamental little bastard anyway.'

The old man was right on that score. Hill House was very temperamental, and his trainer, usually so tough with his horses, indulged him in everything. If Hill House didn't want to school, he wouldn't school. If he wanted to go up one gallop rather than another, that's the one he'd go up.

Hill House came back from his holiday to run at Kempton Park in what is now the Lanzarote Hurdle, but as we were lining up another horse went to kick him, and there was no way he'd jump off. I was booed as I brought him back to unsaddle, but unpopularity was the least of our worries. 'That's buggered things up!' exploded the old man. It was essential for Hill House to have a pre-Schweppes race as he was rusty after his break, so we ran him at Sandown Park a week before the big day. There was no way he could have won as he was far from fully tuned up, but he ran a cracker to finish fourth and the race just put him right.

In that year's Schweppes we also had a good hurdler named Burlington II, and not long before the race I got a call from the old man:

'Josha! You ride Burlington in the Schweppes.'

'I what?'

'You ride Burlington.'

'Who's riding Hill House?'

'Don't know yet. Might not even run him.'

I was terribly disappointed. Burlington was not right at the time and I knew he had no chance, so the next morning I rang back.

'I'm very disappointed not to ride Hill House. Burlington has no chance.'

The final flight in the 1968 Schweppes: Persian War just leads Major Rose and Sempervivum.

'You're quite right, Josha. Find me a good jockey and I'll see what I can do.'

So I phoned Terry Biddlecombe. He agreed to ride Burlington, and Ryan Price was perfectly happy with the arrangement.

Less happy were some Jockey Club officials who thought that they could detect a coup cooking. The old man was told, off the record but on good authority, that if Hill House won the Schweppes the book would be thrown at us, and that we were definitely going to have a long holiday. The fact was that although there had been no cheating there would clearly be some fuss if Hill House showed great improvement in his form, so on the way to Newbury I asked the old man:

'If we win today, what are we going to tell them?'

'TELL THEM THE F***ING TRUTH!!'

By then the Schweppes was the biggest handicap hurdle of the year. Some of the jockeys tended to get carried away, and they went off at a hundred miles an hour. Hill House was not a horse to be hassled, so I let the leaders go and gradually picked them off, hitting the front halfway up the straight. This was probably much too soon, but he was a horse you dare not disappoint once you got him running. He was likely to stick his toes in if he got fed up, but that day, despite looking at the wing of the odd hurdle, he just went further and further clear and won by twelve lengths.

It has been reported that the booing from punters who thought they'd been stitched up started before we reached the final hurdle, but at the end of the race I was not aware of a particularly hostile reception: I knew there was the odd person booing, but mostly I thought I heard cheering.

The old man and I were hauled before the Newbury stewards to explain the improvement in Hill House's form in the week since Sandown, and eventually we were told that the case would be reported to the National Hunt Committee of the Jockey Club.

I don't bet, but a little later I was taken to the end of an eminent Jockey Club member's garden and told that they knew that I had won £46,000 on Hill House – 'Don't argue: we know.'

Before the National Hunt Committee enquiry could take place it transpired that in the post-race dope test Hill House had tested positive to the steroid cortisol. It was a mystery how it had got into his system, so he was sent off to be tested at Newmarket, where it became clear that he produced an unusually high level of cortisone in his body: he became known as 'the horse that doped himself', and after months of being under suspicion the old man was vindicated.

All that fuss over this affair has obscured the fact that the 1967 Schweppes saw the most superb piece of training by Ryan Price, because Hill House was a very highly strung horse and was handled quite brilliantly.

For all those successes, controversial and otherwise, my best ride in the Schweppes came the year after Hill House, when I rode Major Rose in the 1968 running.

Major Rose, who carried eleven stone eight, with favourite Persian War on eleven thirteen, was a class horse on the Flat – he won the Cesarewitch

---

Schweppes Gold Trophy

Newbury, 17 February 1968   *2 miles*

1	Persian War	J. Uttley	9–2 fav
2	MAJOR ROSE	J. Gifford	11–2
3	Sempervivum	T. Jennings	33–1

Also ran: Stubbs II (4th), Black Justice, Sir Thopas, Indamelia, Louis Boy, Le Dauphin, Even Keel, Chambrun, Supermaster, Celtic Gold, Opicola, Retz, Secret Agent, Rackham, Eros Boy, King Of Peace, Sir Nulli, Bric-Brac, Sundew's Nephew, Pikes Fancy, Te Fou, Specify, Hill House, Colonel Imp, Spanish Steps, Kirriemuir, Clarion Call, Spartae, Tudor Times, Tapina

33 ran $\frac{1}{2}$ *length, 2 lengths*

---

the autumn after running in the Schweppes – but he wasn't a natural jumper at all, and used to step over his hurdles. In the Schweppes they went a terrific gallop, and I skimmed along the inside, in mid-division for most of the way until moving up in the straight. At the last flight we were half a length down on Persian War, and this was where Major Rose's great stamina came into play. He battled on so well that he headed Persian War halfway up the run-in (though Persian War's jockey Jimmy Uttley still swears we were never in front) and I thought I was going to win nicely by about half a length. Then Persian War – who the following month would win the first of his three Champion Hurdles – fought back, and all the way to the line it was touch and go. We were beaten half a length, but defeat does not prevent that Schweppes being the best race I ever rode. I timed my challenge perfectly and did everything right – bar winning! **"**

David Nicholson

Mill House in the Whitbread Gold Cup, Sandown Park, 29 April 1967

WHEN DAVID NICHOLSON TELLS YOU what was the race of his riding life, you don't venture to ask whether he's quite sure. 'The Duke' is as famed for his strong opinions and the forthright manner in which he expresses them as for the training expertise which has nurtured such horses as Charter Party, Broadsword, Very Promising, Waterloo Boy, Mysilv, Barton Bank and Viking Flagship and made him champion jumps trainer in the 1993–4 and 1994–5 seasons.

By the time he took out his first trainer's licence in 1968 David Nicholson had already made a considerable reputation for himself as a jump jockey, having been tutored in the riding arts by his father Frenchie, legendary mentor of apprentices including such familiar names as Paul Cook, Tony Murray, Richard Fox, Walter Swinburn and Pat Eddery. Nicholson junior could hardly have come from a background more likely to turn him into a leading rider.

David Nicholson was born on 19 March 1939, and first rode in a race at the age of twelve at Newmarket in April 1951, on a horse named Fairval. The same horse provided him with his first ride under National Hunt Rules – and his first winner – in a selling hurdle at Chepstow on 11 April 1955. In June that year he registered his only riding win on the Flat, on Desertcar at Wolverhampton: the runner-up Paquito was partnered by another precocious young rider, named Lester Piggott.

The close of David Nicholson's riding career overlapped with the early years of training, and by the time he hung up his riding boots in 1974 ('I woke up that morning and for the first time did not look forward to riding, so I knew it was time to stop') he had ridden the winners of 583 jumps races in Britain in addition to that one success on the Flat.

Those 583 winners included several big races, including the Welsh Grand National three years running (Limonali in 1959 and 1961, Clover Bud in 1960), the Schweppes Gold Trophy (Elan in 1965) and the Imperial Cup (Farmer's Boy in 1960). But for David Nicholson the race of his riding life has to be the 1967 Whitbread Gold Cup on the great and glorious Mill House.

Trained by Fulke Walwyn, Mill House – affectionately known as The Big Horse – had won the Cheltenham Gold Cup at the tender age of six in 1963, then suffered defeat by the incomparable Arkle in the famous 1964 race and again the following year. The feeling that he was a great horse desperately unlucky to be contemporaneous with one even greater elicited from the hard-bitten but sometimes sentimental National Hunt fraternity a depth of affection which was apparent every time he raced. It was never more in evidence than in his first race after that devastating 1964 Gold Cup defeat by Arkle, when he just failed to hold off the late challenge of Dormant – to whom he was conceding three stone – in the Whitbread Gold Cup.

Between then and Whitbread time three years later, racing fortune dealt Mill House a measly hand. He won a few more races but never scaled the heights. His spirit was broken, it was said, by too many humiliations at the hands of Arkle. He was certainly due a change of luck.

66 Riding Mill House was like driving a Rolls-Royce. He was a great big horse but tremendously nimble, and a beautiful mover in all paces: he had that feeling of sheer quality which all really great horses have, and was just unlucky to have been in the same generation as Arkle.

Over the years I'd ridden several times for Fulke Walwyn, but Mill House's regular jockey was Willie Robinson, and it was following an injury to Willie that I came in for my first race on the horse, in the Gallaher Gold Cup at Sandown Park in November 1965: since Mill House was such a massive horse, his owner Bill Gollings wanted a substitute jockey with long legs, a qualification which I certainly met.

In preparation for the Gallaher Gold Cup I schooled the horse over fences at Lambourn and then at Newbury, where I had my first experience of his phenomenal strength. At the fourth jump down the far side he simply missed the fence altogether, crashed through and continued quite unconcerned. He could clout a fence so hard he'd break the timber frame, and yet keep galloping.

Fulke Walwyn rarely gave orders before a race, and his suggestion before the Gallaher Gold Cup, in which Mill House was receiving sixteen pounds from Arkle, was simple: down the far side on the second circuit, make every fence count. I did just this, and the big horse winged every one, so that by the far end of the back straight – after jumping the third of the Railway Fences – I was thinking: 'That's stuffed Arkle!' Then all of a sudden, halfway round the turn towards the straight, Pat Taaffe came bump-bump-bumping up alongside us, trying to keep Arkle in check. Once he let him go they shot off into the distance and the race was over. Mill House plodded on to finish third (Rondetto passed us for second), and I have some sympathy with the view that this final defeat by Arkle broke the old horse's heart: it certainly disheartened me!

These defeats at the hands of Arkle – who simply had a different set of gears from that of any other horse – had accumulated a great deal of public sympathy for Mill House, but by the time of the 1967 Whitbread he was ten years old and his greatest days seemed to be behind him. That impression had not been removed by his race before the Whitbread, when I rode him in

'I let him have his way and settled down to enjoy the most exhilarating ride of my life'

the Cheltenham Gold Cup. Arkle had been injured and the chasing world was looking for a new champion, but with no obvious new candidate for the crown it was an open race, with Mill House third favourite in the market behind Fort Leney and What A Myth. Mill House had been suffering back problems and was not right that day, but he travelled well enough on the first circuit and took the lead early on the second, with Terry Biddlecombe and the promising young chaser Woodland Venture upsides us. At the final open ditch Mill House put down when he should have picked up and took a crashing fall. Woodland Venture went on to win.

Willie Robinson was still sidelined by the time of the Whitbread, in which we faced Woodland Venture again, and with a weight concession of three pounds Mill House started favourite at 9–2, with another grand old chaser Rondetto at 5–1 and Woodland Venture third choice at 13–2.

After the Cheltenham experience I was anxious to give Mill House as much sight of his fences as I could, so jumped him off on the outside and tried to settle him: he had won the Gold Cup over three and a quarter miles but was not an out-and-out stayer and I was concerned about his getting the

David Nicholson and Mill House at the last.

Whitbread Gold Cup

Sandown Park, 29 April 1967   *about 3 miles 5 furlongs 18 yards*

1 MILL HOUSE	D. Nicholson	9–2 fav
2 Kapeno	Mr N. Gaselee	100–8
3 Kellsboro' Wood	J. Haine	100–7

Also ran: San Angelo (4th), Woodland Venture, Go-Pontinental, Limeking, Rondetto, La Ina, Monarch's Thought, Solbina, Maigret, What A Myth

13 ran   *$1\frac{1}{2}$ lengths, $1\frac{1}{2}$ lengths*

Whitbread trip of three miles five furlongs. But he took a good hold and by the second fence, coming up past the stands for the first time, had pulled his way into the lead. Despite being so large and long-striding he was not a difficult horse to present at a fence as long as you were definite with him and gave him a clear signal, so I let him have his way and settled down to enjoy the most exhilarating ride of my life.

Down the far side for the first time he measured his fences beautifully, and between jumps I kept taking a tug, trying to slow him down and preserve his stamina for the business end of the race. He felt like a totally different horse from the one I'd ridden in the Gold Cup, and to ride a horse like him around Sandown was an unbelievable thrill.

Coming past the winning post with a circuit still to go Mill House maintained his lead, but the others were bunching up behind me, and John Buckingham – who just a month earlier had scored his sensational Grand National victory on Foinavon – got the sharp end of my tongue when he let his mount San Angelo tap Mill House's heels: I turned round and gave him a right rollicking!

Turning right-handed after the winning post, Terry Biddlecombe and Woodland Venture came up on our outside and started to take us on, which may have distracted my fellow: at the downhill fence Mill House made a bad blunder – birch seemed to be flying all around my head – but as so often just sailed on regardless, and even gained ground in the process. Into the back straight Terry was still trying to get me at it and I was still keeping a strong grip, but the pace was quickening and San Angelo seemed to be going ominously well. We kept the lead over the Railway Fences but I was mindful of what had so deflated Mill House in the Gallaher Gold Cup, and did not want a repeat of the experience. San Angelo was no Arkle but I felt he was about to go past us, so I turned to John Buckingham and yelled at him to take it steady: he was trotting up, and shouldn't make his move too soon. As Buck swallowed the bait and took a pull, I urged Mill House forward and set sail for home. He pinged the Pond Fence and turned into the straight still full of running, jumped the second last well enough and then, with the crowd urging him on, went for the last. He did not meet it quite right and lost a little momentum, and it was then that the full force of his tiredness hit me. The steep climb from the last fence has altered the complexion of many a Sandown chase, and as a desperately weary Mill House set off for the winning post a fresh danger suddenly emerged in the shape of Nick Gaselee and Kapeno, who was making up ground hand over fist.

But Mill House was not going to be denied now, and stuck to his task with tremendous courage, responding to the roaring of the crowd to hold off Kapeno by a length and half.

When we pulled up he was out on his feet – absolutely knackered. He came off the racecourse, and as we started walking up the Rhododendron Walk towards the unsaddling enclosure racegoers started applauding him. The more they clapped, the more he responded, and the tiredness seemed to drain from him, so that by the time he entered the winner's enclosure he was the king being greeted by his adoring public. The reception that day was fantastic – certainly the best I've ever known as a jockey – and made it the most emotional moment of my riding life. **"**

In his autobiography *The Duke*, David Nicholson paid this tribute to The Big Horse: 'Just to sit on Mill House made you feel good. He had a majesty, that horse, which gave you a feeling on his back of reigning supreme. He was certainly the greatest jumper I had the good fortune to ride. It still excites me to try to find one like him to train.'

Declan Murphy

Fragrant Dawn in the Tripleprint Gold Cup, Cheltenham, 11 December 1993

UNTIL 2 MAY 1994, DECLAN MURPHY WAS scarcely a household name. Widely admired as a stylish jockey who after leaving Ireland, where he was born on 5 March 1967 and where he rode his first winner on Prom at Tralee on 21 June 1983, had built up his reputation first with trainer Barney Curley and latterly with Josh Gifford, Murphy had broken into the highest ranks through riding such horses as Deep Sensation and Bradbury Star.

It was on Bradbury Star in the 1993 Mackeson Gold Cup at Cheltenham that he had what was – at least to outside observers – one of his finest riding hours. In the second race that afternoon his mount Arcot had given him such a heavy fall at the second last hurdle that it was scarcely believable to spectators that Murphy was not seriously injured, let alone fit enough to take his ride in as important a race as the Mackeson, the very next event on the card. But he managed to convince the racecourse doctor – and himself – that he was well enough to ride in a race just half an hour after hitting the deck, and duly turned in an extraordinary performance to drive Bradbury Star to victory over Egypt Mill Prince despite suffering an almost literally blinding headache for most of the race.

That episode showed Murphy to be an exceptionally tough as well as skilful rider, but when at Haydock in May 1994 Arcot again took a crashing fall, at the final flight of the Crowther Homes Swinton Hurdle, the immediate issue was not whether the Irishman would ride again that day but whether he would live. So severe were the head injuries he had sustained that the *Racing Post* had the headline 'MURPHY KILLED IN HORROR FALL' set up in case the worst happened. But Murphy rallied while in intensive care and within a few days was back home in Newmarket. Even by the standards of a profession of ultra-durable men and women, it was a miraculous recovery, and it made Murphy front-page news.

On the racing pages, he had long been commanding headlines . . .

"" I have two ways of approaching the idea of the race of my life. It could be the one that gave me most satisfaction, or the one where I've contributed most to the horse's ability to win. The race that gave me most satisfaction has to be the 1993 Queen Mother Champion Chase at Cheltenham on Deep Sensation.

I always considered Deep Sensation a misunderstood horse. He's been called ungenuine, but anyone who thinks that simply does not appreciate a horse's mental make-up. Deep Sensation is the most intelligent horse I've ever sat on, and I've learned more about equine psychology from him than from anything I've heard or read. Admittedly he could appear to be a frustrating horse because to be seen at his best the race needed to be run to suit him. The maximum pace over the minimum trip was what he needed, and when beaten in races where those conditions did not apply he looked as if he hadn't gone through with his effort. He had the highest cruising speed of any horse I ever rode in a race, and – this was what made him so special – could quicken off it. Think of a parallel with a racing car: if Deep Sensation had been a car he'd need to be one gear off overdrive through a race, then he could slip into overdrive and accelerate; but if he was two gears below

Young Hustler and Carl Llewellyn lead Fragrant Dawn and Declan Murphy over the final fence.

overdrive and the pace quickened he would take a long time to gather speed. Also, as he tended to get bored in his races it was vital to keep his interest engaged. In the circumstances he would only be seen in top form in the best races: the better the race was, the better he was.

From the first time he ran in the 1992–3 season I was trying to convince his owners as well as Josh Gifford to go for the Queen Mother Chase. Josh thought I was talking nonsense and wanted to campaign Deep Sensation over three miles – and even the breeder was on the phone to Josh trying to persuade him to run in the Gold Cup!

In November 1992 I got off Bradbury Star to ride Deep Sensation in the H. and T. Walker Gold Cup over two and a half miles at Ascot, which I thought was the perfect race to test my theory about Deep Sensation needing pace throughout the race rather than a sprint finish, and I was proved right: he travelled well throughout the race and took the lead going to the last, then ran on to beat Danny Harrold. Bradbury Star was third.

Come Cheltenham Festival time, Josh still was reluctant to run Deep Sensation in the two-mile Queen Mother, preferring the Cathcart over two miles five furlongs. I had quite a battle to persuade him to go for the shorter race, and the last thing he said to me in the paddock before going out was: 'Good luck, but we should be running in the f***ing Cathcart.'

'I imagined the punters thinking: "What's Murphy playing at?"'

Tactically the race went exactly to plan. I held him up in the early stages, made progress from the top of the hill, challenged the leader Cyphrate going to the last and battled on up the hill to win narrowly. When I returned to the unsaddling enclosure there was no further mention from Josh of the 'f***ing Cathcart': he was very emotional and could hardly talk – he just couldn't believe it.

The 1994 Queen Mother Champion Chase illustrated what could happen to Deep Sensation when tactics backfired. At the top of the hill we were one gear off overdrive – exactly as I wanted – as Remittance Man kept up a strong gallop. I had banked on Remittance Man giving us a lead into the straight, where we would sail by for a second Queen Mother. Viking Flagship, on our inside, was being scrubbed along, and Travado, on our outside, was going well enough, but I was beginning to feel very confident when – disaster! – Remittance Man fell at the third last. Deep Sensation suddenly had to change down from fourth gear to second, and he simply couldn't pick up speed again in time. He finished third behind Viking Flagship and Travado.

And how could anybody think Deep Sensation ungenuine after that wonderful race against Viking Flagship and Martha's Son in the 1995 Melling Chase? [See pages 34–5.] Deep Sensation took a bit of knowing, and it did not help his cause that day that he was ridden by Norman Williamson, who was not familiar with the horse. Furthermore, the race wasn't run to suit him, but he battled on all the way up the straight and was only worried out of it right on the line. If Deep Sensation had one failing it was not that he was ungenuine, just that he lacked instant acceleration.

The Sun Alliance Chase at Cheltenham in 1992 was the greatest race I ever rode in – even though my mount Bradbury Star was beaten by

Miinnehoma. I've never known such a tremendous pace in a race, nor one which was so sustained – we were hell for leather from the moment the tape went up until the final slog up the hill. Some so-called experts thought Bradbury Star wouldn't stay, but he certainly did; and he gave me another wonderful memory – albeit another defeat – when going down by a head to Barton Bank in the King George VI Chase in 1993. Going to the last that day I thought I had the race won, so put him right to jump it carefully. Adrian Maguire on Barton Bank, on the other hand, took a chance and flew it, then just outstayed us up the run-in. Adrian went for a tidy jump at the last on the same horse the following year, but that time it didn't quite come off!

Bradbury Star was never really suited by Kempton. He much preferred Cheltenham, where he won two Mackeson Gold Cups and where the un-dulations mean a horse can take breathers on the downhill stretches before getting back to serious work on the uphill. His second to Miinnehoma was the best performance of his career, and I still love to watch the recording of that finish.

Cheltenham was the venue for the race in which I felt most pleased with my own effort, and which for that reason I have to name the race of my life – the Tripleprint Gold Cup in December 1993 on Fragrant Dawn, who had recently joined trainer Martin Pipe from David Elsworth.

Fragrant Dawn had been a useful performer on the Flat, but he hadn't run since the spring and it was widely believed that he only just got two miles in the highest class over fences, so wouldn't stay the two miles five furlongs of the Tripleprint. Richard Dunwoody, Martin Pipe's stable jockey at the time, had got off Fragrant Dawn in order to ride Egypt Mill Prince for Jenny Pitman, and when Martin rang to offer me the ride I accepted readily, even though I knew little about the horse apart from having seen him race a couple of times. I looked at the form of his recent races and came to the conclusion that he'd been allowed to burn up too much energy: he didn't have a high cruising speed, but was just too keen, and my plan in the Tripleprint Gold Cup was to ride him more quietly to give him every chance of getting the trip. Martin Pipe had been told by other jockeys who had ridden the horse that Fragrant Dawn didn't really stay even two miles, but he assured me: 'If he gets the trip he'll win.'

On the way to the start Fragrant Dawn gave me a marvellous feel – like a Classic horse – and I was not at all bothered when in the early stages of the race the leaders were going along at a furious pace. By the third fence I was all of twenty-five lengths behind them and as we came past the stands I imagined the punters thinking: 'What's Murphy playing at? He hasn't put his horse in the race at all.' What outside observers simply do not under-stand is that you can judge pace only when you get a feel from the horse you're riding. As with Deep Sensation, you come back to the idea of gears, and I knew on Fragrant Dawn that if I could keep cruising in third gear for as long as possible he had such class that he'd be able to quicken away. So the longer we cruised the better, and I just had to ignore what the other riders were doing.

Tripleprint Gold Cup

Cheltenham, 11 December 1993   *2 miles 5 furlongs*

1 FRAGRANT DAWN	D. Murphy	14–1
2 Young Hustler	C. Llewellyn	11–2
3 Freeline Finishing	J. Osborne	20–1

Also ran: Stunning Stuff (4th), Second Schedual, General Pershing, Morley Street, Armagret, Egypt Mill Prince, Another Coral, Brandeston

11 ran   *3 lengths, $\frac{3}{4}$ length*

At the top of the hill the leaders were tiring – as it was perfectly clear they would – and we were starting to creep into the race by cruising along at the same speed while they came back to us. Richard Dunwoody, who would not have been best pleased at getting off the winner of a big race, looked across at me as I passed Egypt Mill Prince on the run to the second last as Carl Llewellyn on Young Hustler kicked on. I was lobbing along while everyone else was hard at work.

This was a luxurious position to be in – one fence to go, full of running, and a horse like Young Hustler to lead me well into the straight. I knew that Fragrant Dawn could quicken whenever I wanted him to, so decided to wait a little longer and took a pull, letting Young Hustler stay ahead. We jumped the last a length down; then I asked Fragrant Dawn to make his move and off we went – past Young Hustler and up to the winning post. Fantastic!

This was an especially satisfying win as although I had never sat on the horse before getting legged up in the paddock I had thought the race through in detail and planned every move – and it all worked out perfectly. The best ride I ever gave a horse. **❞**

Five months after that peak, Declan Murphy was fighting for his life in Walton Hospital. His gradual recovery from his injuries caught the imagination not only of the racing community but of the world outside the sport, and his comeback ride – on Jibereen in the annual Flat vs. Jump Jockeys Challenge at Chepstow in October 1995, for which riders were allotted mounts through a pre-race ballot – was seen as an emblem of the extraordinary resilience of the jump jockey breed. Murphy's first ride back proved a winner, but for him victory was diminished by mean-spirited suggestions that the balloting for rides might have been rigged, and he decided to call it a day, announcing his retirement from the saddle later that month.

Jamie Osborne

Flashing Steel in the Jameson Irish Grand National, Fairyhouse, 17 April 1995

WHEN COMPARISONS ARE MADE BETWEEN the present generation of jump jockeys and their predecessors, one word which keeps coming up is 'style'. Far removed from the push-and-shove, hurl-'em-at-the-fence manner traditionally associated with riding in steeplechases, style in this context signifies a quiet, studied approach, a concentration on presenting your horse at each obstacle and getting the best out of it by persuasion and empathy rather than force. John Francome had it; Richard Dunwoody has it; and no discussion of who is the most stylish of all the current crop is complete without mention of Jamie Osborne.

Born on 28 August 1967, Jamie Osborne rode in point-to-points for trainer Harry Wharton while still at school, before becoming his pupil-assistant and later working for Chris Bell. For Wharton he rode his first winner on Fair Bavard at Southwell on 29 March 1986, and it was while serving as conditional jockey for Nicky Henderson that his talents gained wider recognition, a process which led to the plum job of stable jockey for Oliver Sherwood.

Now firmly established in the top flight of jump jockeys, Jamie Osborne has won many big races – including the 1990 Hennessy Gold Cup on Arctic Call and the 1994 and 1995 runnings of the Tote Gold Trophy on Large Action and Mysilv respectively – and in 1992 equalled Fred Winter's record of winners ridden at the Cheltenham National Hunt Festival when winning five races: the Queen Mother Champion Chase with Remittance Man, the Supreme Novices' Hurdle with Flown, the Arkle Chase with Young Pokey, the Stayers' Hurdle with Nomadic Way and the County Hurdle with Dusty Miller.

His greatest race, though, took place not at Cheltenham but across the Irish Sea, at Fairyhouse.

“ Winning the 1995 Irish Grand National on Flashing Steel gave me as much pleasure as any race I've ever won – even though I didn't immediately like the horse when I started riding him, and never found him straight-forward. Richard Dunwoody had partnered him in his early races, but I took over because Flashing Steel's trainer John Mulhern wanted a jockey who could ride him all through the season, and Richard, then stable jockey to Martin Pipe, could not give that undertaking.

The first time I rode Flashing Steel, in the 1994 Cheltenham Gold Cup, I was tremendously impressed with him, though he was not a particularly comfortable ride: he's very big – you look in front and wonder where his ears are, then look behind and can't see his tail! – and rather awkward in his faster paces. But he finished like a rocket that day to run fourth behind The Fellow, and gave me great hopes about becoming a real Gold Cup horse the following season.

I was soon enjoying the routine whereby I would fly over to Ireland in the early morning, school Flashing Steel at John Mulhern's yard at The Curragh, then catch a plane back to Heathrow in time for racing in the afternoon: all very hectic, but it was great to be part of the team associated with such a good prospect.

It didn't feel quite so great after his first run of the 1994–5 season, in a handicap chase at Navan in December when he was beaten into third behind Bart Owen and River Tarquin. I was disappointed, but put this down to a combination of the heavy going and the race being his first outing. Just after Christmas he went to Leopardstown, where he ran third to Commercial Artist but was beaten by about two fences and finished so exhausted that I had to walk him up the run-in. Suddenly it seemed as if all our high hopes were coming to nothing. He was no longer giving me the feel of a good horse – let alone a Gold Cup winner – and I was beginning to wonder whether I'd made a stupid decision in committing myself to riding him all season.

His next outing was at Fairyhouse, where – thank God! – he restored some of our faith, winning a handicap chase from Lacken Cross. This was a great relief, and encouraged us to keep the Gold Cup on the agenda.

By this time I'd decided that soft ground really didn't suit him, and in the Gold Cup itself I was proved right. On conditions far too soft for his liking he was never travelling at all, and was about to start tailing off when he fell at the second last open ditch. I was seriously beginning to lose faith in the horse, but John Mulhern, who adored Flashing Steel and would never hear a word against him, was adamant that he would eventually prove himself.

After Cheltenham the season appeared to be in tatters, with only a modest Fairyhouse handicap on the scoreboard. But when the ground started drying up in the spring we decided to have a crack at the Irish National, and a schooling session on quite firm ground at Leopardstown renewed my confidence: as I set off to canter down to the first fence he suddenly felt a completely different horse on the better ground, much more like the Flashing Steel I'd ridden in the 1994 Gold Cup.

An additional factor which increased my optimism was the distance of the Irish race: three miles five furlongs. At this trip Flashing Steel would have a real chance of travelling on the bridle rather than – as in the three furlongs shorter Gold Cup – being scrubbed along all the way. On the other hand, the late defection of top-weight Jodami left Flashing Steel carrying twelve stone – a mammoth task in such a competitive race.

'What's that lunatic up to?'

121

The Irish National is run on Easter Monday, when I would normally have plenty of rides in England. But Oliver Sherwood very kindly released me from my home commitments, which in a way added to the pressure: if Flashing Steel flopped again the trip would have been a complete waste of time, and might have cost me winners at a point when I was looking to increase my tally for the season. Any such gloomy thoughts were dispelled as soon as I arrived at Fairyhouse and met up with John Mulhern: he'd never lost confidence in the horse for a moment, and was full of beans that Flashing Steel could pull off a famous victory for his owner Charles Haughey, former prime minister of Ireland and a great follower of racing.

I so much wanted Flashing Steel to show what he was capable of, and decided that the only approach was the positive one – to take the race by the scruff of the neck. This went against John Mulhern's inclination, which was that the horse should be dropped out early on and taken along steadily to give him a chance to warm up. I was beginning to wonder. It might be better to grab the bull by the horns from the word go, and make my horse realise that there was a job to be done. There were eighteen runners, the market leader being Mr Boston, trained by Mary Reveley, and I did not want Flashing Steel to get tangled up in the middle of the field. Put simply, I wanted to get some enthusiasm back into the horse. If we dropped out behind others he might get into a lolloping rhythm and switch off too much, and he's a horse who needs encouragement from his rider: he can be a bit awkward at his fences and needs helping all the way round. My plan was to bounce him out of the gate, engage his interest, and see what happened.

I lined up on the tape, gave him a few digs in the ribs, and away we went. Over the first few fences we were right up in the front rank, and I could imagine John Mulhern in the stand thinking: 'What's that lunatic up to? Twelve stone, three miles five furlongs, and he's in the lead!' But I knew what I was doing – getting Flashing Steel travelling on the bridle, and when horses travel well they jump much better.

After vying for the lead early on I let the race develop, trying to hold my position along the rails just behind the leaders. Flashing Steel was not foot-perfect – he was very sloppy at one of the early fences and missed it badly – but on the whole he was jumping well. His attitude towards jumping is part of what makes him a less than straightforward ride: he tries to be careful but does so in an awkward way, and he needs working on to keep him awake. He's the sort of horse who will exhaust his jockey because you've got to do half the running for him.

Coming past the stands with a circuit left he was still going well, but then made another sloppy mistake. At that I started to get annoyed with him, so gave him a couple of belts with my whip, which put him back on the bridle. By now the field was thinning out. We'd been lucky enough to have a trouble-free run, but it was time to start thinking about the business end of the race. Although one or two were starting to make their moves down the far side, I didn't want to commit just yet, and decided to bide my time. At the fourth last Mr Boston unseated Peter Niven, and at the third last Rust Never Sleeps went on.

At that stage I felt I had everyone's moves covered. Flashing Steel was still travelling very well, but with twelve stone on his back I didn't want to wind him up too soon as I thought he might not be able to finish that well. So it was still a case of biding my time. Then suddenly the picture changed as Rust Never Sleeps in a moment went from being a length or two up to being all of fifteen lengths ahead of me. I was worried, but knew that Rust Never Sleeps was perfectly capable of drying up, so we still had a chance. Kicking and shoving, I kept Flashing Steel after him, and slowly we started to cut back the deficit. Approaching the second last, with Rust Never Sleeps still well clear, I realised we were completely wrong, so just sat still for a split second to allow my fellow to put himself right. I gained no ground at that fence and if anything was now farther back. I started to think we needed a miracle.

We set sail for the last with Rust Never Sleeps in our sights but looking uncatchable, and as we neared the fence I made a conscious decision: go straight for the last no matter what, don't look for a stride. Flashing Steel is not really the sort of horse on whom you can take such risks as he needs all the help going, but when you're looking sixty grand in the face it's better to fall at the last than jump it carefully and finish runner-up.

He met it spot-on, jumped quickly and landed running; but we were two lengths down on Rust Never Sleeps and the run-in at Fairyhouse is short. Landing over the last it was still odds against our winning, but those odds started to tumble as we set off in pursuit of the leader, and halfway up the run-in we were surely odds-on. Rust Never Sleeps began to stop and Flashing

Jamie Osborne and Flashing Steel in full cry.

Jameson Irish Grand National

Fairyhouse, 17 April 1995   *3 miles 5 furlongs*

1 FLASHING STEEL	J. Osborne	9–1
2 Rust Never Sleeps	T. J. O'Sullivan	50–1
3 Feathered Gale	F. Woods	10–1

Also ran: Belvederian (4th), Force Seven, Royal Mountbrowne, Antonin, Ebony Jane, Nuaffe, Captain Brandy, Loshian, Bishops Hall, Jassu, Belmont King, Sullane River, The Committee, Mr Boston, Scribbler

18 ran $\frac{1}{2}$ *length, 20 lengths*

Steel found overdrive, thrusting out his long neck – useful in a tight finish – and clawing his way past the leader to win by half a length.

As we came into the winner's enclosure, to a wonderful reception, Charles Haughey was there to lead in his horse. But where was John Mulhern, to whom this result meant so much? He was nowhere to be seen, and it transpired that he'd been sitting on his own in the racecourse stable yard – crying and thanking God. When he arrived in the paddock to greet his winner he could hardly speak – though he was able to tell me later that when he saw me take Flashing Steel to the head of affairs early on he had indeed thought I'd taken leave of my senses.

The presentation was pretty special, as Charles Haughey received the trophy from the current Irish prime minister John Bruton. Fairyhouse is in Haughey's constituency and he fought hard to save the course when it was under threat a few years ago, so he's immensely popular locally.

Even were he never to win another race, this was Flashing Steel's day, and I, just a small part in a perfect result, was whisked along on a tide of emotion. I went up to Charles Haughey's box, where the celebrations included a little boy – about five years old – standing on a table singing 'Molly Malone'. It was wild!

Then the winning connections, with plenty of others in tow, set off on what I can only describe as a pub crawl. I'm no expert on Irish politics, but it struck me as unusual, to say the least, to be part of a binge with a former prime minister all the way from Fairyhouse to The Curragh, with Haughey announcing at every pub we entered: 'Free drinks for everyone all night!' I still haven't a clue how or when I got back to Dublin, but I was awake enough to ride the following day.

Whether at Taunton, Cheltenham or Fairyhouse, the biggest buzz I get from riding a winner is to see how much pleasure it gives others, and I've never seen people – racegoers as well as immediate connections – more delighted than they were that day. 🙮

Mick Fitzgerald

Rough Quest in the Martell Grand National, Aintree, 30 March 1996

'**S**EX WILL BE AN ANTI-CLIMAX AFTER THAT.' Never was the excitement of a Grand National-winning jockey better expressed than by Mick Fitzgerald's description of the experience of winning the Aintree race in 1996 on Rough Quest. The National had provided 'the best twelve minutes of my life' – to which his fiancée Jane Brackenbury offered the appropriate response: 'He's never lasted twelve minutes in his life!'

The peach of a ride which Mick Fitzgerald gave Rough Quest during just over nine of those twelve minutes came as no surprise to anyone who had followed his career since he moved in 1988 from his native Ireland to England and made his name as a rider of great finesse – principally through his association with Lambourn trainer Nicky Henderson, whom he joined at the beginning of the 1992–3 season.

Fitzgerald was born in Cork City on 10 May 1970. The riding skills given early expression on a black pony named Daisy, whom he described as 'lethal', were channelled through apprenticeship with Irish trainers Richard Lister and then John Hayden before he crossed to England, where he rode his first winner on Lover's Secret in a conditional jockeys' selling hurdle at Ludlow on 20 December 1988. Curiously, Fitzgerald had never ridden a winner in his native country until partnering Rough Quest to land the Castlemartin Stud Handicap at Punchestown in April 1995, the month after the same horse had given him his second Cheltenham Festival victory in the Ritz Club Chase; his first Cheltenham Festival winner was Raymylette in the 1994 Cathcart.

His debut Grand National, however, proved a severe disappointment: he rode Tinryland for Nicky Henderson in 1995, and the pair did not survive the first fence.

On his second ride in the Aintree marathon, however, things worked out rather better.

66 I first rode Rough Quest in a handicap chase at Nottingham in February 1995. We came third, but I was tremendously impressed by him, and told his trainer Terry Casey when we returned to the unsaddling enclosure: this horse is a machine. The week before the 1995 Cheltenham Festival I rode him in a two mile five furlong chase at Wincanton, where the leader Menebuck made a mistake at the last which left me a length clear. Rough Quest tied up in front, Menebuck rallied and we were beaten three quarters of a length. I was beginning to learn about this horse, and when Terry Casey and Rough Quest's owner Andrew Wates asked me whether we should go for the three mile one furlong Ritz Club or the shorter Mildmay of Flete at the Festival, I strongly suggested the longer race.

I'm glad I did. It was, as usual, a very competitive event – sixteen runners and a strong pace. Coming down the hill last time round I was absolutely running away, and had to put Rough Quest into the bottom of the second last to stop him getting to the front too soon. He'd been jumping like greased lightning – as quick as any hurdler I'd ridden – and the knack was to hold up his challenge until the last possible minute. The horses in front of me were all stopping, so I had to take it up – still on the bit – just before the last. On landing I was afraid he'd stop, so gave him a little squeeze and he accelerated up the hill to win so easily I could hardly believe it – and so easily that I told Terry Casey on coming back in: this horse will be in the first three in the Gold Cup.

He then went and won at Punchestown, and early in the 1995–6 season we started to map out his campaign. I was keen that he should be aimed at the King George at Kempton as I was convinced that the race would suit him, but Terry was not sure he'd be good enough. Meanwhile, after falling on his reappearance at Cheltenham, his first big target of the season was the Hennessy Gold Cup at Newbury. I was suspended following some nonsense over bypassing a hurdle at Taunton, and the ride went to Jamie Osborne. I stressed to Jamie that the way to ride Rough Quest was to drop him right out, but the horse put in such a bold show of jumping down the far side on the second circuit that he let him go on, and going to the last they were caught by Couldnt Be Better. To be fair to Jamie, he did not know Rough Quest well, but the horse had a hard race and I was desperately disappointed that he'd not been able to prove himself as good as I knew he was.

I was reunited with him for the Betterware Chase at Ascot in December, before which he'd had a recurrence of the muscle enzyme problem which had bothered him for a while. He didn't really feel right, though he would certainly have won but for hanging to his left after the last and letting Unguided Missile and Richard Dunwoody get back at us and beat us a neck.

Woody rode Rough Quest on his next outing at Leopardstown as I was claimed to ride in England – they fell at the fourth last when going very well – and kept the ride when winning the Racing Post Chase at Kempton in February since I was committed to partnering Amtrak Express for Nicky Henderson. But Terry Casey had assured me that the ride on Rough Quest was mine whenever I was available, and I was back on board for the Cheltenham Gold Cup. I was convinced that he wouldn't be out of the first three, and coming down the hill last time, getting closer and closer to the leaders, I began to think we'd win. In the straight One Man fizzled out and there was only Imperial Call to catch, but after the last Rough Quest had no more to give and he was beaten four lengths. I felt that with softer ground he might have got closer, and it greatly annoyed me when some so-called experts used the proximity of Rough Quest to Imperial Call to knock the form of the race. The simple fact is that in a truly run race – which the Gold Cup was – Rough Quest is a very good horse indeed.

Immediately after the Gold Cup the question arose as to whether he would go on to the Grand National. The week before Cheltenham, Terry Casey had told me that the Gold Cup would be his last race of the season, so I accepted a National booking for Bavard Dieu, trained by Nick Gaselee. On the Sunday morning after the Cheltenham race I saw on the teletext that Rough Quest would after all be running at Aintree, so, well aware that Woody had not at that stage got a National ride, was immediately on the phone to Terry. He wasn't at home, but the thrust of the message I left was clear enough: if Rough Quest runs, I ride! At lunchtime Terry rang. It was really Rough Quest himself who had brought about the change of heart: he was so well after Cheltenham, absolutely bouncing, that they would now aim for the National – and if he ran, I would indeed ride.

I extricated myself from my commitment to ride Bavard Dieu – which did not make me hugely popular with Nick Gaselee – and concentrated on how I would ride the National.

One ride in the race, and that ending at the first fence, did not make me much of an expert, but I had dreamt of winning the National for as long as I could remember, and to have such a major chance was a fantastic opportunity. The weights had been allotted before Rough Quest had run in the Racing Post Chase and the Gold Cup, and he had been given ten stone seven pounds, which on his Gold Cup form made him an absolute certainty providing he got round. If he took to the race he would win: simple as that.

I drove up to Liverpool with my father. We came off the M6 by Haydock Park to make our way across towards Runcorn, where we were staying, and every single traffic light between the motorway and the hotel was red – which I took as a very bad omen!

There are famous stories of jockeys who indulge in riotous nights and then go out and ride the race of their lives in the National, but my style has always been to take it quietly. The night before the race Dad and I had a quiet dinner together, then the following morning I got up, had a little break-fast, and watched *The Morning Line* on Channel Four – where I was bemused to see my great idol John Francome slagging off Rough Quest with comments to the effect that the horse would only get the trip in a horse-box! Normally John is very acute, but that sort of knocking didn't bother me: the more I thought about it – and I thought about it a great deal – the more convinced I was that Rough Quest had to win. Get over the first three fences, get him settled and enjoying himself, and there'll be no problem. Hunt round on the first circuit, and on the second, when the field is start-ing to thin out a bit, put him gradually into contention. As always I consid-ered every other horse in the race: which jumps to the left or right, which is a sketchy jumper, and so on. You need to keep all that information in your mind, especially in a race like the National, and after a good look at the

> 'The more I thought about it, the more convinced I was that Rough Quest had to win'

nature of the opposition I knew which ones I wanted to avoid having around me. Keep in round the bends to save ground, fan out on the straights and get a nice clear path. Get him settled and let him see what he's doing. And if he likes it, he'll win.

Rough Quest didn't turn a hair during the parade and before I knew it my faith in the horse was about to be put to the test. He jumped off well, met the first fence long and cleared it beautifully. At the second he saw a big stride and jumped very steeply, but came down so sure-footed I thought: perfect! He popped the third, the big open ditch, and my confidence started to soar.

Two of the horses I had not been keen to have around me – Far Senior and Brackenfield – were in fairly close attendance, so I kept Rough Quest towards the outside of the field going down to first Becher's in the hope of staying clear of interference. He jumped Becher's well but kicked himself in the chin on landing, and I was still worried that I was behind too much rubbish, a sure recipe for trouble. So on straightening up after the Canal Turn I pulled him out a little to let him see what he was doing, and after he'd jumped Valentine's beautifully I let him bowl along.

That stretch of the Grand National course from the Canal Turn to the Melling Road is wonderful to ride – dead straight, bags of room, with big but beautifully built and inviting fences. At this stage of the race the pace slowed a little from the clip they'd been going for the first mile, and the leaders bunched up. Rough Quest was starting to pick up the bridle again and get keen, and as we made for the thirteenth, the first fence after the turn towards home on the first circuit, I could hear the roar of the crowd in the stands as they tensed for the run towards the Chair fence. Rough Quest jumped both the thirteenth and fourteenth quite brilliantly, and as we made for the Chair, with its huge ditch on the take-off side, he was going too well for his own good. He often tends to rush at open ditches, and I had to get him back on his hocks: whoa! whoa! He touched the board guarding the ditch on the ditch but jumped this huge fence superbly, then pinged the water jump, and out we went for the second circuit.

I tucked him in round the bend but he grabbed the bit and started to run on, which is just what I did not want to happen, and as we straightened up to cross the Melling Road again and go for the seventeenth – the first on the second circuit – the field fanned out and I pulled him to the outside. Once he saw daylight he wanted to go again, so I had the dilemma of how to keep him back and still give him enough freedom to jump properly. He took the seventeenth so well that he made up too much ground again. Take a pull: whoa! whoa! He was always tremendously quick at his jumps and could make two or three lengths over the average staying chaser, but with him now getting up among the leaders I had to slow him down. So I let him get in tight to the eighteenth, which was just the job: he lost momentum and dropped back to where I wanted him to be. This was the way to ride him at this stage of the race: on landing over the fence, put my hands down on his neck and let him settle, whereas had I picked him up he'd have gone charging off again.

He got a little too close to the one before second Becher's, but generally everything was going perfectly, and approaching Becher's I pulled him out to give him plenty of daylight. He jumped the fence alongside Woody on Superior Finish, popped over the next and the Canal Turn, and after straightening up it was time to get serious.

This is the stretch of the National which makes everybody's water tingle. As I had gradually moved up from towards the back of the field I knew that there was nothing which was going to come from behind me, and all the dangers were in front. Young Hustler was leading, with Sir Peter Lely on the inner and Three Brownies right up there with them, and Encore Un Peu, ridden by David Bridgwater, and Life Of A Lord still going strongly. Of these Young Hustler and Encore Un Peu were my main dangers, and now I had to keep close enough to them without letting Rough Quest make too much progress too soon. I was very happy to see Young Hustler in command as I knew he'd give us a good lead and wouldn't die in front.

We crossed the Melling Road and made back towards the racecourse proper, at which point I saw Bridgy on Encore Un Peu look round to see how the opposition was going. It struck me that Bridgy had a lot more horse under him than I'd thought, and now it was important to move up alongside Young Hustler and keep Encore Un Peu in view, so that he didn't get too good a run on me. At the same time I had to be mindful of not getting there too soon, so going to the second last I again took a pull. Rough Quest

Encore Un Peu is clear and out of the picture, but Mick Fitzgerald has the leader in his sights as Rough Quest, tracked by Young Hustler, skips over the last.

Martell Grand National

Aintree, 30 March 1996 $4\frac{1}{2}$ miles

1	ROUGH QUEST	M. A. Fitzgerald	7–1 fav
2	Encore Un Peu	D. Bridgwater	14–1
3	Superior Finish	R. Dunwoody	9–1

Also ran: Sir Peter Lely (4th), Young Hustler, Three Brownies, Life Of A Lord, Antonin, Over The Deel, Vicompt de Valmont, Captain Dibble, Riverside Boy, Over The Stream, Greenhill Raffles, Into The Red, Lusty Light, Sure Metal, Deep Bramble, Son Of War, Party Politics, Chatam, Rust Never Sleeps, Bishops Hall, Wylde Hide, Bavard Dieu, Brackenfield, Far Senior

27 ran $1\frac{1}{4}$ *lengths, 16 lengths*

jumped that one well, but now Bridgy kicked on. I had him covered, yet knew that I had to leave myself something to make up, as if Encore Un Peu made a mistake at the last I'd be in front too soon. So I stayed about five lengths behind him, jumped the last really well, then set off in pursuit. Rough Quest often hung left under pressure and now tried to seek the assistance of the far rail as Bridgy drove Encore Un Peu to the right towards the elbow. In the back of my mind was the fact that Rough Quest was now in unknown territory as far as his stamina was concerned: he'd been hacking all the way round, was still not out of second gear and had an electric turn of foot, but I couldn't assume that he'd get back if the other had gone too far in front.

Going to the elbow I made to challenge Bridgy up the inner, but he closed the door and forced me go towards the stands side, then rolled out, pushing me further to the right as we straightened for the line. Rough Quest was full of running but hanging to the left for the inside rail and leaning on Encore Un Peu, so I tried to yank him off to the right. In a matter of about three strides he'd shot past and found the rail, then ran on strongly to the line to win by a length and a quarter.

My immediate feeling on pulling up was one of relief – that my faith in the horse had been vindicated, and the race had gone exactly to plan. Well, not quite exactly, and after Rough Quest's crossing over I assumed there would be an enquiry, though I was very confident of keeping the race.

I was a little less confident when I saw Terry's face as he came to meet us, and it was clearly not as straightforward as I'd thought. People said later that the enquiry took the gloss off being led back in between the two police horses – one of the great moments for a National-winning jockey – but in truth I was just overcome with the whole experience. Enquiry or no enquiry, it was a fantastic feeling, and I wanted that walk to last for ever.

On dismounting I assured Andrew Wates that there would be no problem with the enquiry, but when I got into the stewards' room I wasn't quite so certain, as the first piece of film I saw showed Bridgy dramatically snatching up his horse as Rough Quest cut across towards the rail – a bit of gamesmanship worthy of any Premier League striker, and definitely a penalty! Of course, he was only doing his best for connections, and he'd ridden a marvellous race. He said to me later that it would not have felt right had he been given the race, but he was at least spared that, as after several nail-biting minutes it was announced that the stewards had let the placings stand.

The celebrations had to wait until I'd ridden in one more race that afternoon, and then I went off to find my Dad. The look on his face just made the day for me: he was proud as punch. I took him to the weighing-room for a glass of champagne, and then we set off for the journey home to Faringdon – where friends had erected balloons and a huge sign outside my house: 'WELL DONE, MICK – WHAT A QUEST!' Jason Titley, who lives three doors down from me and who had won the 1995 National on Royal Athlete, phoned his congratulations from hospital – where he was being treated for broken ribs following a fall at the first fence from none other than Bavard Dieu.

It was late by the time we got down to Franco's in Faringdon for a proper celebration with all the other local jockeys. The following day I drove down to Terry's yard near Dorking for the traditional post-National get-together, and then that evening went to London for the Jockeys' Association annual awards – the Lesters. Quite a weekend!

Winning the National is something I'd thought about ever since I was a kid. When you consider all the famous jockeys who never won the race – John Francome, Scu, Graham McCourt, Josh Gifford, Stan Mellor, Jeff King, Jonjo, David Nicholson – you realise what an elite band you've joined when you're lucky enough to do so.

I got a lot of stick over my remark about its being better than sex, but it seemed like nothing could ever better the way I felt then. It was a dream come true. **99**

Michael Roberts

Mtoto in the Coral-Eclipse Stakes,
Sandown Park, 4 July 1987

Michael Roberts is the only South African ever to have become champion jockey in Britain, and his total of 206 winners when lifting the title in 1992 made him only the second Flat jockey since Gordon Richards to cross the 200 barrier. (The first was Pat Eddery with 209 in 1990.)

Born on 17 May 1954 in Cape Town, Michael Roberts spent five years at the South African Jockeys' Academy from the age of fourteen, and rode his first winner on Smyrna at the Pietermaritzburg Turf Club at Scottsville on 30 August 1969. He was fifteen. While serving his apprenticeship with trainer Herman Brown he became champion jockey in South Africa for the first time in the 1972–3 season and proceeded to repeat the achievement in all but one of the next eleven years: the last of his eleven South African championships came in 1983–4, and in 1982 he became the first jockey ever to ride over 200 winners in a South African season.

He came to Britain for the 1978 Flat season, when he rode twenty-five winners – the first of them Pakeha at Ayr on 3 April. But it was when he returned in 1986 that he really started to make his mark, and it took only until 1994 to notch up his 1,000th British winner.

The first top-class horse to put Michael Roberts on the British riding map was Mtoto, winner of the Eclipse Stakes in 1987 and 1988 and the King George VI and Queen Elizabeth Diamond Stakes in 1988, and a narrowly beaten second to Tony Bin in the 1988 Prix de l'Arc de Triomphe. English Classic success came with Mystiko in the 1991 Two Thousand Guineas and Intrepidity in the 1993 Oaks, and other notable victories with the likes of Indian Skimmer, Opera House, Lyric Fantasy, Terimon and Barathea.

❝ In some ways the most memorable race I rode was the 1993 Oaks on Intrepidity. This was the year when I was retained jockey for Sheikh Mohammed: I won the Irish Two Thousand Guineas on his colt Barathea, but Intrepidity, trained in France by André Fabre, was my first English Classic winner in his colours.

I'd never sat on Intrepidity – a big, well-made filly – until the parade ring before the Oaks, but knew that she'd done enough to justify second favouritism in the race, having won the Prix Saint-Alary at Longchamp the previous month. In the paddock André Fabre told me that she had a tremendous turn of foot and I was to be careful not to hit the front too soon – and the lad leading her up told me she was very sleepy. This did not augur terribly well, and going the reverse way round to the start, as we reached the mile and a quarter gate, she nearly dumped me.

In the race itself she was off the bridle from the word go, and very sluggish in the early stages. As we crossed over to the inside rail after taking the right-hand bend a furlong from the start she was squeezed up, clipped the heels of the horse in front and pecked very badly, shooting me out of the saddle and on to her head, then throwing me back into the plate as she righted herself. From then on I was pushing and shoving her, smacking her with the whip to try to get her interested. Never mind hitting the front too soon – I couldn't get her anywhere near the front!

On the run down to Tattenham Corner she was still way back, with me smacking her and urging her on but our cause looking fairly hopeless, then once we hit the straight she started to come good and run on. She collared the front-runners Royal Ballerina and Oakmead well inside the final furlong and won going away by three quarters of a length.

An amazing performance, but a nightmare of a ride: I can't think of many Epsom Classic-winning jockeys who've had the whip out well before Tattenham Corner!

But the race which on balance meant the most to me has to be Mtoto's first Eclipse Stakes in 1987.

A late-developing son of the 1967 Eclipse and King George winner Busted, Mtoto, trained at Newmarket by Alec Stewart, ran just once as a two-year-old – third in a maiden race at Yarmouth. I was impressed with him the first time I ever rode him at home, and some of his work on the gallops was unbelievable.

I first rode him in a race on his debut as a three-year-old, in a mile and a quarter maiden race at Salisbury, when he started odds-on but was run out of it close home by a horse of Guy Harwood's. Next time out he won a maiden at Haydock, then stepped up considerably in class in the King Edward VII Stakes at Royal Ascot, where he finished fifth behind Bonhomie. On that form he looked a certainty for a small race over one mile three and a half furlongs at Yarmouth in July, but couldn't quicken and came second to Magic Slipper. We'd worked him on the Limekilns gallop at Newmarket with Then Again, a very good miler of Luca Cumani's: Mtoto went past Then Again like he was standing still, which helped me persuade Alec that bringing him back in distance might be the answer. He ran next in the Andy Capp Handicap at the big York August meeting, where he carried nine stone seven pounds and ran on well to come second to My Generation, and ended the season with a good fourth behind Sure Blade in the Queen Elizabeth II Stakes at Ascot.

Overall, his form as a three-year-old was a far cry from the sort of level which would have set us thinking about the Eclipse or King George, but we

'Mtoto was right up my alley!'

knew that as a son of Busted he'd need time to reach his peak, and expected him to improve considerably at four. His first outing of the 1987 season was in the Brigadier Gerard Stakes at Sandown Park's evening meeting in May. He was up against Allez Milord, a very good horse who had been narrowly beaten in the Japan Cup the previous November and had won the Gordon Richards Stakes at Sandown very easily on his reappearance. Allez Milord was odds-on favourite and Mtoto 16–1, but Mtoto took it up with a brilliant burst of acceleration inside the final furlong and I had only had to push him out to hold off the favourite. He then went to the Prince of Wales's Stakes at Royal Ascot. I was suspended and had to miss the ride, but under Richard Hills the horse again produced a fine turn of foot to win by two and a half lengths. Next stop Sandown Park.

The Eclipse Stakes is the first big race of the season when the top middle-distance three-year-olds come up against their elders, and in 1987 the traditional clash of the generations was perfectly set up by the presence of Reference Point, who had led all the way to win the Derby under Steve Cauthen and appeared to be a very high-class colt indeed.

But Reference Point was not the only top-class rival Mtoto faced. There was also the great French mare Triptych, who on her last outing had won the Coronation Cup, Bellotto, who had finished third in the Derby, and Milligram, winner of the Coronation Stakes at Royal Ascot.

Mtoto was an easy horse to ride but he could pull very hard in a race (he never pulled on the gallops) and the key to our tactics was to drop him out early and get him to relax. Once Mtoto was tucked in behind horses he tended to relax, though he would panic a little if others were close behind him.

Impressed, like everybody else who had seen it, by Reference Point's victory in the Derby, Alec had a characteristically pessimistic approach to the race: he's won the Derby, how can we beat him? I, on the other hand, was very confident. I knew that Reference Point would ensure a strong gallop and I knew that Mtoto had an amazing turn of foot. The race was set up for him.

We needed to break slowly so that he would drop in behind other horses and keep travelling on the bridle until his turn of foot would come into play, and the race went perfectly. Mtoto missed the kick and got tucked in as Steve Cauthen and Reference Point made the running. They scorched along the back straight, but the quicker they went the better it suited me.

Media Starguest, who was in the race as a pacemaker for Triptych, took on Reference Point down the back and we stayed in the rear, biding our time. As we made our way round the final bend I gave Mtoto another inch of rein and a little tap on the shoulder to test how he was going. Jeez! – I couldn't believe it! He stepped up a gear effortlessly, so I brought him back on the bridle and turned him off again. Given the speed we were going, he was extraordinarily relaxed, and I was confident that I could get to Reference Point whenever I wanted.

Coming round into the straight Mtoto came hard on to the bridle. I half went with him, then waited again, then, once we'd straightened up for home, eased him out slightly. Reference Point was still going very strongly in the lead and I checked to see how Triptych was travelling: she could take her time to pick up, but when in the mood would fly, and I didn't want to get past Reference Point and then be caught by her. I seemed to have her covered, so it was time to get after the Derby winner. Just inside the final furlong we were upsides and I thought: we've got him! Mtoto was wonderfully brave – both horses were – and with Steve on the rail and me on the outer we had a tremendous duel. Mtoto gradually forged ahead, then close home Reference Point came back at us until just before the line Mtoto asserted and went on to win by three quarters of a length.

It was a great race, but for me had a special significance, as a jockey needs association with a good horse for his career to develop, and Mtoto really put me in the limelight in Britain. From then on there was no looking back.

Mtoto missed the King George later in the month on account of the soft going, and after running fourth in that year's Arc returned to Sandown in

'A tremendous duel': Mtoto (right) and Reference Point hammer and tongs.

Coral-Eclipse Stakes

Sandown Park, 4 July 1987 $1\frac{1}{4}$ miles

1 MTOTO	M. Roberts	6–1
2 Reference Point	S. Cauthen	evens fav
3 Triptych	A. Cruz	4–1

Also ran: Bellotto (4th), Milligram, Gulf King, Sharp Noble, Media Starguest

8 ran $\frac{3}{4}$ length, $1\frac{1}{2}$ lengths

1988 and won the Eclipse again – this time from Shady Heights, after another great duel. He went on to run in the King George, and despite recurring doubts about whether such a good-actioned horse could act on soft going – I was always confident that he would – won well from Unfuwain.

He ran a wonderful race in the Arc, just failing to pin back Tony Bin, but that day he simply didn't feel quite as good as he had on King George day: he didn't sparkle, and was a little flat-footed. At his best – as in the Eclipse against Reference Point – he would pick up instantly, but in the 1988 Arc he didn't. Having tracked Tony Bin through, I was about to make my challenge but had to wait a couple of strides while Village Star on my outside got out of my way – and after that Mtoto was never going to get to the winner.

But he was a wonderful horse to partner, the ideal sort for me. I love to ride from behind, and with his spectacular turn of foot Mtoto was right up my alley! **99**

Graham Bradley

Bregawn in the Tote Cheltenham Gold Cup, Cheltenham, 17 March 1983

BY THE TIME GRAHAM BRADLEY WON THE Champion Hurdle on Collier Bay in March 1996 he had become, at thirty-five, one of the grand old men of the jump jockeys' changing room. After an early career highlighted by success in the 1983 Gold Cup on Bregawn at the age of twenty-two but then clouded by what he himself described as an 'image problem', in 1991 Bradley became stable jockey to trainer Charlie Brooks, a role which provided the perfect showcase for the talents of one of the most elegant jump jockeys of his generation.

The son of trainer Norman Bradley, Graham Bradley was born in Wetherby on 8 September 1960. He joined Tony Dickinson as conditional jockey and it was for Dickinson that he rode his first winner, Talon in a novices' hurdle at Sedgefield on 11 March 1980 (the same afternoon that Sea Pigeon won his first Champion Hurdle). When Tony Dickinson was succeeded by his son Michael, Bradley became established as second-string rider to this powerful yard behind stable jockey Robert Earnshaw. For Michael Dickinson, and later Michael's mother Monica, Bradley rode many big winners in addition to Bregawn (on whom he won the 1982 Hennessy Gold Cup en route to his Cheltenham triumph), including Sabin Du Loir in the 1983 Sun Alliance Hurdle, Badsworth Boy in the 1983 Castleford Chase, Righthand Man in the 1984 Welsh National and Wayward Lad in the 1985 King George VI Chase. He also won the 1985 Irish National on Rhyme 'N' Reason and the 1986 Welsh National on Stearsby.

If the great Cheltenham victories on Bregawn and Collier Bay are two candidates for the race of Graham Bradley's life, a third is the remarkable ride he gave Morley Street in the Martell Aintree Hurdle on Grand National day 1993.

❝ Morley Street was the best hurdler I've ridden – a great character, and a very good horse indeed. I'd ridden him in the Champion Hurdle that year, when he was well beaten by his full brother Granville Again, and it felt to me as if two miles at Cheltenham might have been a little on the sharp side for him. Two and a half miles at Aintree, on the other hand, was ideal: pan-flat, nice long home straight, and a run-in of about a furlong and half.

By this time Morley Street had the reputation of being a bit of a dog, but I never thought of him like that. The trouble was that he had to be ridden very delicately, as he idled in front, and the trick in the Aintree race was to produce him at just the right time. He was only third favourite – Granville Again was odds-on, and Flown, who'd started favourite for the Champion Hurdle, was well fancied – so there was little pressure, and Morley Street's trainer Toby Balding suggested I just go out and enjoy myself.

In the race Morley Street jumped like a buck and settled beautifully: never before in my life had I been on a horse that was travelling so well. All the way round I bided my time, and up the straight he was just cruising. Going to the last we were about a length behind Richard Dunwoody on Flown, with Peter Scudamore and Granville Again on the inner and apparently beaten, and it was an incredible feeling to be going to the last in a championship race knowing that I had two gears left. I knew I had them all beaten, and there was no point in going on and risking Morley Street stopping in front, so I was thinking: I'd better wait here. After the last Flown was flat out, and I was planning to pop Morley Street's head in front on the line and win by a neck or half a length. There's a path across the track about seventy-five yards from the line, and I thought I'd hold him up and just go on once we'd crossed that. I was going that easily that nothing could go wrong, but then Granville Again suddenly threatened to spoil it. Scu had been very clever, switching from the inner to the outer, and I had a bit of a dilemma. Flown was stopping and coming back to me, I was reining back Morley Street in order not to get in front too soon, and now Granville Again was starting to stay on. As soon as I saw Scu I knew I'd have to press the button, so I thought, 'Here we go!', gave my fellow one smack, and he lengthened his stride instantly, running on to win by a length and a half.

Collier Bay was a much more straightforward ride, and winning the Champion Hurdle on him was one of the great moments of my riding life – not least because of the shenanigans which preceded it.

Alderbrook had won the Champion Hurdle brilliantly in 1995 and was widely fancied for a repeat, but when Kim Bailey's stable jockey Norman Williamson was injured the Cheltenham ride became a matter of much speculation. A few of the boys were sidelined, some of the others were committed elsewhere. Jamie Osborne might have come in for the ride but had already agreed to ride either Collier Bay for Jim Old or Mysilv for Charlie Egerton, and when Kim Bailey asked me to go and school Alderbrook (who had not run over hurdles since the previous year's Champion) on a Sunday morning in February I was very flattered and very honoured – and very hopeful that this would lead to my getting the ride at Cheltenham.

So far, so good.

The evening before the planned schooling session Dean Gallagher – who earlier in the season had won the Hennessy on Charlie Brooks's Couldnt Be Better when I had ridden Black Humour for the stable – had a birthday party in a hotel near Newbury. Having an important appointment with

Alderbrook the following morning I was dithering about whether to go, but figured that I should be able to get back to my house near Wantage and then have a decent night's sleep before getting up in good time to be on the gallops by ten. So I decided to go. All the boys were there and we had a hell of a time – such a good time, in fact, that I ended up drinking a trifle more than I'd intended. About half past one in the morning I got a taxi back home and put myself to bed. My girlfriend Amanda – who had not gone to the party – got up at seven o'clock as she had to drive to Birmingham that morning, and set the alarm clock for nine-fifteen before leaving the house.

I've always been a heavy sleeper – I once slept through a Los Angeles earthquake which measured 8.6 on the Richter Scale – and after a few drinks find it very difficult to come to, so I was completely dependent on that alarm clock doing its stuff . . .

It was ten twenty-five when I woke up, to one of the worst feelings I'd ever had in my life – a mixture of embarrassment and panic. I leapt out of bed and paced around for a couple of minutes before plucking up the courage to call Kim Bailey, who I knew would be up on the Lambourn gallops waiting for me, on his mobile phone. I explained how the alarm had not gone off, offered him my profuse apologies, and said I'd be there in ten minutes. Had there not been another jockey on the gallops they might have waited for me, but as luck would have it John McCarthy was up there, and he'd been commandeered to take Alderbrook through his schooling session. Kim said not to worry: go back to bed. So I did.

It transpired that there had been a power cut in my village at 9 a.m., which had disposed of any chance of my electric alarm clock going off at the right time, but this was little consolation, and although I was hoping I might be given another chance, Richard Dunwoody became available and got the ride on Alderbrook, winning on the horse on his highly impressive reappearance at Kempton Park before partnering him in the Champion Hurdle.

This saga left me without a Champion Hurdle ride, but Jamie Osborne asked me to stand by for whichever he turned down out of Mysilv and Collier Bay. I'd ridden Mysilv in the previous year's Champion and she'd given me a great ride – the best I'd yet had in the race – to finish fifth behind Alderbrook. I'd won on Collier Bay, trained by Jim Old, at Sandown Park earlier in the season, and knew that he was a good tough horse whose over-all form might have been underestimated but who needed soft ground to be seen at his best.

The weather was the key to Collier Bay's chance, and when the weekend before the race the going seemed to be drying up, Jamie plumped for Mysilv, leaving me on Collier Bay. Then the day before the race it started to rain, and continued through the night, so that the going on Champion Hurdle day was officially good to soft. It was too late for Jamie to switch, and I knew that I had a great chance.

Collier Bay had started at 25–1 when winning at Sandown in January, since when he had been ridden by Jamie to win the Irish Champion Hurdle at Leopardstown – a victory which had gained him less credit than it

'Bregawn was always a very odd horse'

139

deserved, with all the attention being focused on Danoli's run into third place on his seasonal reappearance. I thought I had a great chance of getting in the first four at Cheltenham – and Jim Old was convinced that Collier Bay had come on ten pounds since Leopardstown – though I did not seriously think that we could beat Alderbrook, who had been exceptional in the race in 1995 and had so impressed at Kempton.

After all the convoluted lead-up, the Champion Hurdle itself does not need much describing. Collier Bay jumped brilliantly, and I spent most of the race on Mysilv's quarters as she made the pace. Coming down the hill and approaching the second last I pushed Collier Bay up into the lead – and as I passed Jamie I heard him curse himself: 'F***! F***! F***! F***!' He'd chosen the wrong one . . .

Off the final bend I kicked on and made for the last. He met it perfectly, responded to a couple of smacks and charged up the hill. Three quarters of the way up the run-in he started to get tired, and at that moment I could tell from the barrage of noise from the crowd that something was closing on us. I did not turn round to see who it was but kept my head down, gave him one more smack and rode for the line. After pulling up the first horse I saw was Alderbrook.

'Were you second?', I asked Woody. When he said yes, I leant over and gave Alderbrook a heart-felt pat. To land a Champion Hurdle in those circumstances, and so long after my first big Cheltenham win on Bregawn, gave me one of the best feelings I've had in my riding life. Kim Bailey went out of his way to congratulate me in the weighing-room afterwards, and there were no hard feelings over the alarm clock incident.

Collier Bay was the better horse on the day – end of story!

The real hero of the 1983 Gold Cup was not a horse but a trainer – Michael Dickinson, who trained the first five home at his yard at Harewood in Yorkshire.

I'd ridden Bregawn in the 1982 race, when we'd finished second to another Dickinson star, Silver Buck, and since Robert Earnshaw would be riding Silver Buck through the 1982–3 season and both horses would be aimed at the top staying chases, I kept the ride on Bregawn.

From the moment he came into the yard, Bregawn was always a very odd horse. He was tiny but built like a battleship, and although small to look at did not feel small to ride. He had a real mind of his own: he'd plant himself and be impossible to budge, and would even get down into a ditch and root himself there. The lad who looked after him was amazingly patient, and would play with the horse's ears to keep him interested before he'd consent to come out. But his run in the Gold Cup was one of the bravest I've ever known, and although he was often mulish at the start, once the tapes went up he was like a lion. He wasn't a natural jumper, but Robert Earnshaw had done a wonderful job schooling him.

We had a great time that season, winning a small race at Newton Abbot and the Rehearsal Chase at Chepstow before landing the Hennessy from another Michael Dickinson-trained horse, Captain John. Bregawn was beaten in his next two races but in order to put him right mentally and sweeten him up for the Gold Cup he was then sent to Hereford for a small race in which he was such a certainty that there was no betting. He was left at the start but still won by a distance, and to give him a decent school round under those circumstances was a brilliant ploy on Michael's part.

The five Dickinson runners in the Gold Cup – Bregawn (who started favourite), Silver Buck (ridden by Robert Earnshaw), Wayward Lad (Jonjo O'Neill), Captain John (David Goulding) and Ashley House (Dermot Browne) – represented nearly half the eleven-runner field. Of the rest, Combs Ditch, Fifty Dollars More and Brown Chamberlin were the only realistic dangers to the Harewood team.

Michael was a true perfectionist, and before the race walked the course with all his five jockeys. As always, he knew about every other runner – its form, how it would be ridden – and advised us on how to ride the course. An ex-jump jockey himself, he had a tremendous knowledge of the different circuits – where to make up ground, where to have a breather, which line was best to take – and always passed this on to his jockeys. He had an incredible brain, and was a wonderful trainer to ride for. On Gold Cup day he gave each of us, as always, five or six sets of instructions to cover every eventuality which might occur in the race, with the proviso that we could improvise were none of these eventualities to come about – which is just what happened!

'Bregawn pulled his way ahead.'

Tote Cheltenham Gold Cup

Cheltenham, 17 March 1983 $3\frac{1}{4}$ miles

1 BREGAWN	G. Bradley	100–30 fav
2 Captain John	D. Goulding	11–1
3 Wayward Lad	J. J. O'Neill	6–1

Also ran: Silver Buck (4th), Ashley House, Richdee, Midnight Love, Combs Ditch, Fifty Dollars More, Brown Chamberlin, Whiggie Geo

11 ran   *5 lengths, $1\frac{1}{2}$ lengths*

Bregawn had tended to be difficult at the start of his races, and in the Gold Cup was led in by Michael's travelling head lad: he got a flyer, so that was one potential problem out the way. The plan had been for Ashley House to make the running, but he did not go quick enough in the early stages, and the 500–1 outsider Whiggie Geo took it up. The pace still wasn't fast enough for my liking, so going away from the stands on the first circuit I let Bregawn, an out-and-out galloper rather than a speed horse, increase the tempo a little, and before I knew it he was making the pace. I just let him bowl along, and thereafter never saw another horse until, going to the last fence, Captain John appeared on my right, with Wayward Lad trying to mount a challenge up the inner on my left. At the last Captain John was practically upsides, and I knew that we had to go long: if he put in a short one he'd lose too much ground, so I fired him in, met it on a long stride, landed running and away we went. I just kept batting away with my stick and Bregawn pulled his way ahead. He was five lengths clear at the line.

I knew that Captain John had come second – David Goulding was convinced he'd have won had the horse not made a mess of the fence at the top of the hill! – and that Wayward Lad was third, but it was not until we got back to the unsaddling enclosure that I learned that Michael's horses had filled the first five places: an amazing achievement.

The race left its mark on Bregawn psychologically, and he was never the same afterwards. He became increasingly mulish; in the following year's Gold Cup he wore blinkers, but they had little effect, and he tried to pull himself up before finishing way behind Burrough Hill Lad. By the time of the 1985 race he was being trained in Ireland, but his behaviour had deteriorated further and he was tailed off when refusing at the last.

But in his prime Bregawn was a very, very good horse, and of all the races I won, that 1983 Gold Cup still gives me the greatest pleasure. I'd gone against instructions but my judgement was proved right, and I don't think I've ever ridden better. **"**

Michael Kinane

Belmez in the King George VI and Queen Elizabeth Diamond Stakes, Ascot, 28 July 1990

WHO IS THE BEST FLAT JOCKEY IN THE WORLD – Jerry Bailey? Frankie Dettori? Pat Eddery? Pat Day? Debate on such a theme is as diverting as it is pointless, but there is one current rider whose international record displays an unparalleled span of achievement: Michael Kinane. Who else has ridden the winner of the Derby, the Prix de l'Arc de Triomphe, a leg of the US Triple Crown, and the greatest Australian race, the Melbourne Cup? Since crashing into the big time when winning the Arc in 1989 on Carroll House, Kinane has rapidly established himself as one of the great jockeys of the present international era of modern racing.

Son of Tommy Kinane, who won the Champion Hurdle in 1978 on Monksfield, Michael Kinane was born in Tipperary on 22 June 1959. An early indication that he would be following his father into the saddle came when at the age of ten he took part in a fancy dress parade in Killenaule as Lester Piggott – dressed in breeches and silks and carrying a saddle. He served his apprenticeship with trainer Liam Browne at The Curragh, and rode his first winner on Muscari at Leopardstown on 19 March 1975, becoming champion apprentice in Ireland in 1978. In 1984 he joined trainer Dermot Weld, and the same year was Irish champion jockey for the first time, repeating the feat another seven times up to 1993.

Mick Kinane really hit the headlines on the first weekend of October 1989, when on the Saturday he won the valuable two-year-old race the Cartier Million at Phoenix Park on The Caretaker, trained by Dermot Weld, and on the Sunday landed the Prix de l'Arc de Triomphe at Longchamp on Carroll House, trained by Michael Jarvis.

Thus catapulted into the international spotlight, Kinane has not looked back since. He won his first English Classic on Tirol, trained by Richard Hannon, in the 1990 Two Thousand Guineas, and in June 1990 won the Belmont Stakes at Belmont Park, New York, on Go And Go – the first European-trained horse ever to land a leg of the US Triple Crown. The following month he took the King George VI and Queen Elizabeth Diamond Stakes on Belmez. (His second ride in the King George – on King's Theatre in 1994 – produced a second victory.) In that 1990 King George, Kinane rode Belmez as Henry Cecil's stable jockey Steve Cauthen had chosen to partner Old Vic, and the tabloid label of 'super-sub' stuck to Kinane with a vengeance after the 1993 Derby. With the choice of owner Khalid Abdullah and trainer Henry Cecil's two runners, Pat Eddery had plumped for hot favourite Tenby. Mick Kinane took the mount on the less fancied Cecil–Abdullah runner Commander In Chief – and landed his first Derby.

Later in 1993 Mick Kinane played a leading role in one of the greatest racing achievements in Turf history when partnering Vintage Crop to become the first horse trained outside Australasia to win the Melbourne Cup, the most important, historic and prestigious event in Australian racing.

    " Carroll House was originally Walter Swinburn's ride, but Walter was not available to partner the colt in the Irish Champion Stakes at Phoenix Park in September 1989 and I came in for a very useful spare. We won from Citidancer and I kept the ride for the Prix de l'Arc de Triomphe.

On the form book it was hard to give Carroll House a major chance in Paris, but unlike most of his rivals he went very well in soft going, and on the day the rain started coming down in torrents. I'd never ridden in the Arc before but I knew well enough the theory about the best way to ride the course, and the golden rule: never make your move until the final straight.

Sitting in the weighing-room before the race as the rain continued to bucket down I began to think we had a shout, and by the time we entered the stalls I was almost optimistic. We were drawn towards the outer, which suited me very well as I wanted to keep him clear of trouble in the early stages, and for most of the trip the race went without any bother at all. I kept him a little wide and had a lovely clear run, took up a position going into the 'false straight' one turn from home, then sat quietly until we'd straightened up – at which point I got into the horse and went for everything. Carroll House quickened up wonderfully well, taking the lead about a furlong and a half out but then edging to the right towards the filly Behera. He won by a length and a half, though celebrations had to be put on hold while the stewards looked into the possibility that we had caused interference when Carroll House drifted. I had a few frightening moments before the all-clear was given.

I then rode Carroll House in the Japan Cup, where on ground much too firm for him he was well beaten.

Go And Go got to his famous victory in the Belmont Stakes almost by chance. After winning a couple of races in Ireland as a two-year-old he went across to Laurel Park, Washington, for the Futurity, one of the big American juvenile races. (I was unable to ride him there on account of commitments in Ireland.) The Futurity was scheduled to be run on turf, but an overnight deluge made the grass track unraceable and it was switched to dirt: Go And Go won by a head, and thereafter Dermot Weld knew that the horse had a real future on the artificial surface. I rode Go And Go when he returned to the USA for the Breeders' Cup Juvenile at Gulfstream Park: he could finish only eighth, but with great foresight Dermot decided that if the horse did not make the grade for the European Classics there were always the top American races to aim for.

In the event Go And Go showed us that he was unlikely to be good enough for the Derby, when fourth in the Derrinstown Stud Derby Trial at Leopardstown on his second appearance as a three-year-old, and Dermot decided to go for the Belmont. In the hope of livening him up a little after that disappointing display at Leopardstown we fitted a visor for the American race, and he turned in a fantastic performance.

I'd never ridden in a Triple Crown race before and the atmosphere on Belmont Stakes day was wonderful. Perhaps it got to Go And Go, as he was firing on all cylinders that day. He was drawn towards the inside and I was happy enough to sit in behind the leaders in sixth or seventh place going down the back stretch; then, about five furlongs out, I asked him to make a forward move. He responded so effortlessly that it was clear I had a great deal of horse under me, still on the bridle, and I thought: this is mine! I waited until the top of the home stretch before asking him for his effort, and he quickened in incredible style, coming right away from the others to win by the huge margin of eight and a quarter lengths. It was a staggering achievement.

'I knew in my own mind that I had something to prove to myself'

His next race was the Travers Stakes at Saratoga, and this time the home jockeys, who had not taken much notice of us before the Belmont, thought they might stitch me up a little. Coming out of the stalls we were hit hard by horses around us, and Go And Go laid his ears back and just took off – so fast that I couldn't get him to settle at all. He ran too freely and just ran out of petrol in the straight, finishing unplaced. In the Breeders' Cup Classic at Belmont Park he was struck into early in the race and finished last, and then stayed in the USA to join the stable of D. Wayne Lukas in California.

Go And Go brought me one of my greatest moments, but there's no doubt that my favourite horse has to be Vintage Crop – so durable, with so much heart, a really versatile horse and a true battler.

Going to the Melbourne Cup in November 1993 with him was a whole new ballgame for myself and Dermot Weld, and most of the people in Australia thought we were demented, not running the horse for six weeks before the race: many of the local runners have their prep race on the Saturday before the Cup itself on the Tuesday!

Vintage Crop was well weighted but Dermot did a very good job of playing down his chance and keeping things low-key, thus avoiding the hype into which an Irish challenge for Australia's most famous race could so easily have fallen. I was starting my usual winter stint in Hong Kong, and flew down to Melbourne the day before the race. Although I'd never previously ridden in a Melbourne Cup I'd watched films of the last twenty or so runnings to get an impression of how the race – a two-mile handicap – tended to be run, and realised that it could be very rough and very tight. As soon as I arrived in Melbourne I went and walked the course to get its shape and nature imprinted on my mind.

The other European challenger that year was dual Ascot Gold Cup winner Drum Taps, ridden by Frankie Dettori, and my plan was to get in behind Frankie and try to avoid the scrimmaging which would be inevitable in a field of twenty-four runners. I got a good run all the way round as the early pace proved fairly steady, and then about six furlongs out the tempo was stepped up. Turning into the straight I still had seven or eight lengths to make up on the leaders, but Vintage Crop was going so well within himself that at that stage I knew I'd win. Drum Taps was not going well enough to pose a threat and the Australian horses were all flat to the boards. About a hundred yards out we got to the front, and were three lengths to the good at the line. An amazing result.

That Melbourne Cup capped what had been a pretty good 1993, the highlight of which before Melbourne had been winning the Derby on Commander In Chief.

Like most jockeys, I always make a point of walking a course with which I'm not familiar, and the first time I ever walked round Epsom, as an apprentice, I had a real shock! The turns and gradients are extraordinary, and I found myself thinking: do they really run the Derby round *here*? Yet it is the nature of the course which makes the Derby a unique test for horse and rider, and winning on Commander In Chief was a huge thrill.

The old one-two for Sheikh Mohammed as Belmez (no. 13) and Old Vic battle it out.

Henry Cecil had two in the race, and a couple of weeks beforehand had asked me to ride whichever of the pair Pat Eddery declined. After Tenby had won the Dante Stakes impressively he became all the rage for the Derby, and Pat elected to ride him. This was understandable, but Henry never really

146

considered Commander In Chief – who had not run at two but was unbeaten in three races as a three-year-old – his second string, and when I went to Newmarket to ride the colt in a piece of work ten days before the race I was impressed not only by the horse himself but also by his trainer's obvious high regard for him.

Tenby started odds on for the Derby, with Commander In Chief second favourite at 15–2. I knew that my fellow would stay, and the plan was to be quite handy in the early stages while keeping him out of the inevitable scrimmaging. Sure enough, there was a fair amount of jostling early on, and since Commander In Chief was such an inexperienced horse I thought it wise to keep him back – slightly further back than ideally I would have liked – to avoid trouble.

At Tattenham Corner we were about seventh, then once we got into the straight I asked him to move up, and he responded so well that I knew he'd win – especially when I glanced across at Pat on Tenby and saw him pushing the panic button! Commander In Chief took the lead a quarter of a mile out and thereafter never looked in the slightest danger, galloping on well to win by three and a half lengths from Blue Judge.

I never rode him again, Pat being back on board for the Irish Derby, which he won from Hernando, and the King George, in which he was third behind Opera House and White Muzzle.

Winning the Derby gave me as much of a kick as any victory I'd enjoyed to that time, yet the race which meant the most to me has to be the 1990 King George on Belmez, since that win seemed to mark a passage for me from being a 'lucky' rider to one who could prove himself in the top company and on the biggest occasions.

The first time I sat on Belmez was in the paddock before the race, but I knew enough about him to see that he had a major chance, even against the likes of Sheikh Mohammed's other two runners, Old Vic – who had won the French and Irish Derbies the year before and had been officially rated top three-year-old of 1989 – and In The Wings. Belmez had won his first race as a three-year-old at Newbury and then landed the Chester Vase from subsequent Derby winner Quest For Fame. But he sustained an injury in that race which for a time looked like bringing his racing career to a premature end until he made such a full recovery that he was able to take his place in the Irish Derby – where he ran well to finish third behind Salsabil and Deploy.

Steve Cauthen had the choice between Old Vic and Belmez, and Henry Cecil asked me to ride the other. Steve chose Old Vic, which put me on Belmez, but with the going on the firm side there was doubt about Old Vic's running, even up to the afternoon of the race. Had Old Vic been withdrawn Steve would have got on to Belmez and left me on the sidelines, but you can't win the big races unless you make yourself available and I decided to take the risk. I'm glad I did, as it was decided at the very last minute that Old Vic would take his chance.

Even though I'd never ridden him before, I soon got the feel of Belmez – a burly, sturdy horse who turned out to be what you might call a very

---

King George VI and Queen Elizabeth Diamond Stakes

Ascot, 28 July 1990 $1\frac{1}{2}$ miles

1	BELMEZ	M. J. Kinane	15–2
2	Old Vic	S. Cauthen	4–1
3	Assatis	M. Shibata	16–1

Also ran: Cacoethes (4th), In The Wings, Terimon, Charmer, Husyan, Sapience, Legal Case, Limeburn

11 ran   *neck, $1\frac{1}{2}$ lengths*

---

physical ride. He would hang to the left and to the right, and had to be forced to do things, rather than adjusting naturally to a race: as an aid he wore a 'pricker' – a small brush attached to the bit – to stop him hanging to the left.

I knew Belmez would stay well and decided that the simple tactic would be to track Steve on Old Vic, who was a great galloper: as long as I had him in my sights I would always be handy enough. At the turn into the home straight Old Vic was in the lead, about two lengths ahead of Belmez, with Cacoethes and Assatis breathing down our necks. We fought off the other two and when we got to Old Vic halfway up the straight I thought we'd win handily enough, but the older horse would not give in and we had a tremendous battle through the final furlong, with Belmez sticking his nose in front inside the final fifty yards and winning by a neck.

Steve and I had both ridden pretty forceful finishes – with today's whip rules we'd probably have got a good few days off! – but it had been a great tussle, and although I didn't ride Belmez again (Steve rode him when he won the Great Voltigeur at York and was unplaced in both the Arc and Japan Cup), at the time the King George was a result of huge significance for me. I knew in my own mind that I had something to prove to myself – had to show that I could compete with the big boys on level terms and ride as well as any of them. In that sense the 1990 King George was a watershed in my career. **"**

Kevin Darley

Celtic Swing in the Prix du Jockey-Club, Chantilly, 4 June 1995

A YEAR IS A LONG TIME IN RACING. THE 1994 Two Thousand Guineas gave Kevin Darley – long admired and respected as one of the most experienced and skilled grafters in the jockeys' room – his first ride in an English Classic, on 100–1 shot Piccolo. They finished among the backmarkers. The 1995 Two Thousand Guineas saw Darley basking in the limelight as rider of Celtic Swing, most talked-up horse of the last twenty years and hot favourite to win the Classic as the first leg of an intended bid for the Triple Crown. That the sky-high hopes entertained for Celtic Swing's three-year-old career did not materialise was deeply disappointing to racing as a whole as well as to the colt's connections, but for Kevin Darley the breakthrough, after seventeen years of honest endeavour, had been made. He had joined the top flight.

Born in Tettenhall, Staffordshire, on 5 August 1960, Kevin Darley served his apprenticeship with Reg Hollinshead, riding his first winner on Dust-Up at Haydock Park on 5 August 1977 – his seventeenth birthday. The following year he was champion apprentice with seventy winners.

In the early 1990s Darley's career stepped up a gear. Riding the great sprint handicapper Chaplins Club led in 1991 to a retainer from the gelding's owner Peter Savill, who had horses in several different yards, and the winners started to flow. On 23 July 1993 Darley rode five in one day (one at Carlisle then four at Ayr), and the same year topped 100 winners for the first time, ending the season with 143 as runner-up to Pat Eddery in the jockeys' championship. In 1994 his total of 154 gave him third place in the table behind Frankie Dettori and Jason Weaver, and in 1995 his score of 148 again put him in the runner-up berth, behind Dettori. On 28 April 1995 he rode his 1,000th domestic winner in the shape of Busy Banana – owned by Peter Savill – at Carlisle.

But in Kevin Darley's career one horse stands handsome head and shoulders above all the others.

" Celtic Swing had been bred by Lavinia, Duchess of Norfolk, whose daughter Lady Herries trained for Peter Savill, and it was on a visit to her stables at Arundel with Peter in the spring of 1994 to ride a two-year-old he was interested in buying that I first clapped eyes on him. A magnificent dark brown, almost black, colt, he stood out on looks and had an air of real class – he was the best-looking two-year-old I'd ever seen – and when he worked alongside me I was very impressed. On dismounting after the gallop I asked Lady Herries about the colt, then quickly got into the car with Peter and told him: you've got to buy that horse! Shortly afterwards I went down to Arundel again to ride Celtic Swing himself and check him over, and then Peter duly bought him.

His first race was in July at Ayr. He won well – by four lengths from Eight Sharp, with Chilly Billy, who went on to win the Gimcrack Stakes, back in fourth. But he hadn't travelled in the race quite as fluently as we'd hoped he would, and gave signs of being backward: he took his time to get going, but once I rattled the reins at him and got him to concentrate it was simply a matter of how far he would win. After that race I said to Peter: this fellow could be quite good.

Celtic Swing then went to Ascot in October for the Hyperion Stakes. He won so easily that I started to pull him up three quarters of a furlong out, but he still broke the two-year-old course record! We'd gone into that race thinking he could be something special, and it was a relief as well as a thrill to discover that we had not been wrong.

Next stop was the Racing Post Trophy over a mile at Doncaster. Celtic Swing had never really had a race, having won easily enough at Ayr and positively doing handstands at Ascot, and before the Doncaster race Peter said: don't be frightened to give him a smack or two just to let him know what the job's all about. The ground was softer than he'd raced on before and we were a little unsure how he'd go on it, but we need not have worried. He was always travelling exceptionally well, and when early in the straight I decided it was time for him to show what he was made of, I kicked him in the belly and gave him a couple of smacks to keep him going – and he shot so far clear of the others that I simply couldn't believe it: I had to look round twice to convince myself that it was real! He won by twelve lengths, an astonishing margin for a Group One race.

That win in the Racing Post Trophy illustrated Celtic Swing's quality – a very high cruising speed and the ability to quicken off it, which can disappoint horses behind. When you're cruising that quickly those behind you tend to think that you're going too fast and will stop, so if you can then find a length or two by quickening off that pace they use up their resources trying to get to you, and it sickens them off. Celtic Swing was a relentless galloper with a stride that covers a huge amount of ground, and when I asked him to quicken I could feel him change down a gear and open up: not a sense of instant acceleration, rather of that mammoth stride just getting longer and longer.

He'd been an outstanding two-year-old – a freak – but for me whatever he achieved as a juvenile was always going to be a bonus, as he wouldn't come to himself physically until he was three. All through the winter the talk was of what he might achieve at three – even that he could be the first horse since Nijinsky in 1970 to land the Triple Crown. Such talk did not put particular pressure on me as his three-year-old debut approached. As far as I was concerned, pressure went out the window at Doncaster: he'd proved himself that day, and my confidence in the horse was sky-high.

It was a very long winter, and I couldn't wait to get back on him. I first rode him in February, and as he wasn't doing very much on the home gallops we used to take him to different places – Guy Harwood's gallops, for instance, or Ian Balding's – to keep him interested.

He seemed to have trained on well, and although he had not grown a great deal from two to three he had filled out in all the right places and was now a magnificent horse to look at. Despite what the looks and the gallops tell you, you really don't know how well a horse has trained on until a race, and there was a little apprehension in the camp going into his first race of the season, the Greenham Stakes at Newbury. He was about eighty per cent fit and won very handily from Bahri with the rest of the field way back, and it was a great relief to know that he had indeed trained on. It was also exciting, as we were well aware that there was more work to be done to get him fully fit, and there was clearly a great deal left in his tank.

'Celtic Swing had proved himself the champion we'd long known him to be'

Between the Greenham and the Guineas we started to get serious with him, and as he reached the peak of condition our main worry was the state of the going at Newmarket. My agent Nick Babington, who lives in Newmarket, walked the course practically every day during the week leading up to the race and reported back. On Guineas morning I walked the course myself and found the going good enough, but it was a scorching hot day and by the afternoon the sun had baked the ground.

In the race itself he was hampered when making his forward move, then I asked him to quicken two furlongs out. But going down into the Dip he got unbalanced: I was trying to push him out but he was coming back under me, and it took him a stride or two to sort himself out and get running again, allowing the French horse Pennekamp to come with a tremendous run on our outside and go half a length up. When we hit the rise Celtic Swing was still feeling the ground a little, but then he found his stride and started clawing back Pennekamp, failing by only a head.

It was a disappointment to be beaten, but he'd run a marvellous race and my confidence in him had not been dented. I was convinced that in any case he would excel at distances longer than the mile of the Guineas, and if anything the Newmarket trip would have been too sharp for a horse who had won over a mile as a two-year-old.

With defeat in the Guineas, Triple Crown aspirations had evaporated, and it was no longer automatic that Celtic Swing would go to Epsom for the Derby. My immediate impression after Newmarket was that the colt would not act on the notoriously difficult Epsom gradients, and Peter tended to agree: we should consider supplementing him for the French Derby, the Prix du Jockey-Club, at Chantilly. It was a gut-wrenching choice for him to make, and as decision time came closer I found myself swaying one way and the other. Naturally for an English jockey the Derby at Epsom is *the* race to win. But there was no point in going for it with a horse who probably wouldn't act on the track – and, much worse, might jar himself up and ruin the rest of the season. He had got unbalanced running downhill in the Guineas, and another indication of how uncomfortable he could be going downhill struck me one morning at Lady Herries' gallops. We were walking through the woods down a track which must be 1 in 10. Celtic Swing was leading the string at the top of the hill – but by the foot the rest of them had gone past me. He just did not like walking downhill.

Initially, however, he was trained for Epsom. We took him to Lingfield Park – a course, like Epsom, with a steep downhill sweep to the left-handed turn into the straight – for a private gallop. He worked well, but the going there was perfect, and word from Epsom was that despite watering the ground was likely to ride much faster on Derby Day than Celtic Swing would have liked. I went down and walked the track, and was not encouraged. Peter did likewise, and we then made a joint decision: go to Chantilly. This was certainly the right course to take; had he gone to Epsom he could have done himself a hell of a lot of damage.

I'd never ridden at Chantilly before, but was confident that as long as the ground was to Celtic Swing's liking he would win – no question! It was,

Celtic Swing holds off Poliglote (rails) and Winged Love (no. 4).

however, annoying to hear people questioning my own ability to go there and do the business on the horse, and I knew that I had something to prove, to the critics if not to myself.

My wife Debby came over with me – moral support! – and while she went off to find some lunch I walked the track with Nick Babington. I was quite happy with the ground, which sported a good covering of grass, and was just a little concerned to see the slightly downhill run into the final bend: it would be important to keep my position there and not risk losing it through Celtic Swing's becoming unbalanced.

After walking round I returned to find Peter lunching in a large marquee and clearly in a nervous state.

'Have you walked the course?' he asked.

'No need,' I replied, hoping that a little levity might lighten the tension: 'There's a little map of it here in the racecard!'

Before the race the heavens opened, thus making the ground much more in Celtic Swing's favour, and going down to the start my confidence, already high, was rising. I knew my horse well, had a shrewd idea of how the others would run, and had worked out a game plan which simply involved avoiding getting into a position from which I could not get out. I didn't want to make the running, but didn't want to get too far behind either – and at all costs I wanted to avoid getting in the box seat in third or fourth, close up but hemmed in with nowhere to go, which often happens in races in France, where there tends to be a slow pace early on. The only thing on my mind was: get where you want to be and stay there.

Celtic Swing was even-money favourite in an eleven-runner field which included useful performers such as Classic Cliche, who had won the Dante Stakes and would go on to take the St Leger, Poliglote, who had been second in the Prix Hocquart, and Winged Love, who had won a Listed race at Longchamp on his most recent outing.

We were drawn towards the outside, which was fine by me, as however he jumped off I had the option: if he jumped well I could take him back, if not I could kick him back in without other horses dropping in on top of me. In the event he broke well enough, and I dropped in behind Walter Swinburn on Classic Cliche all along the back until, passing the Chateau on the run towards the home turn, we moved round Classic Cliche and slotted in behind the leaders. Celtic Swing was travelling very well indeed, and I knew that if we were to be beaten it would have to be by a very good horse: I was hack cantering!

Yet there was one tiny doubt niggling at the back of my mind. This was Celtic Swing's first ever attempt at a mile and a half, and the possibility was there that he might not find enough in the closing stages to last home. So I decided to sit still for a little while longer and nurse him until the race really got going. As we straightened up for home another horse made a short-lived challenge on the outside before dropping away, and Freddie Head and Poliglote on the inside rail suddenly seemed to find a gear. My first reaction to this was that Poliglote would give Celtic Swing a lead for as long as I wanted – then I thought he was going to lead me too far and I might not

Les Emirats Arabes Unis Prix du Jockey-Club

Chantilly, 4 June 1995 $1\frac{1}{2}$ miles

1 CELTIC SWING	K. Darley	evens fav
2 Poliglote	F. Head	81–10
3 Winged Love	O. Peslier	5–1

Also ran: Classic Cliche (4th), Flemensfirth, Diamond Mix, Affidavit, Rifapour, Walk On Mix, Indian Light, Commoner

11 ran $\frac{1}{2}$ *length, short head*

be able to get past him at all! Inside the final quarter mile it was time to get serious with Celtic Swing, so I gave him a kick: he responded and we took the lead, at which point he started to idle and let Poliglote keep on at him up the rail while Winged Love mounted a furious late flourish on the outside. I still felt I had plenty in the tank, however, and we were not hard pressed to hold off Poliglote and win by half a length. Winged Love was a short head further back in third.

Celtic Swing had proved himself the champion we'd long known him to be, and I was absolutely over the moon. Pulling him up, I tried to gather my thoughts, gave him a pat down the neck, then turned to make our way back to the stands – from where an ecstatic party of his connections was rushing towards us. Once we got near the crowd the cheer was unbelievable – and I remember commenting later that the British crowd should give Pennekamp just such a welcome should he win the Derby at Epsom on the following Saturday. The reception was unforgettable.

I learned subsequently that the French jockeys were not very pleased with me as in the rush to get to the post-race press conference and then charge off to catch my flight home I'd omitted to do the traditional thing and buy champagne for the changing room. This omission was put right – after a fashion – when I got to Thirsk the next day and made sure the lads there got a crate of bubbly!

Celtic Swing was now back on course for a summer campaign at the highest level, but his season came to a premature end in the Irish Derby at The Curragh.

On seeing him that day I thought he looked to have run up a little light behind the saddle, but generally he seemed in immaculate condition, and cantering across to the start was perfectly happy and relaxed, though the ground was again a little lively for him. He travelled well enough in the early part of the race, and turning for home was going every bit as well as he had been at Chantilly, but at the point when he came off the bridle there was nothing there, and he failed to quicken, finishing eighth behind Winged

Love. This was clearly not his true running, and it turned out that he had injured himself – perhaps when clipping the heels of Classic Cliche early in the race, or even, according to the vets, as long ago as the Guineas.

It was a real kick in the backside to have that happen, but you have to accept that sort of reverse as part and parcel of racing. What could not be taken away from me was the unforgettable experience of riding Celtic Swing at his peak. To go into top races riding a star like him gives you tremendous confidence in yourself – which in turn is transmitted to the horse. No doubt about it: Celtic Swing made me a better jockey.

He also gave me, at Chantilly, my greatest race – and my only regret was that my father, who was my biggest fan and who died in 1993, was not there to see it. It was the proudest moment of my life. 99

Charlie Swan

Danoli in the Sun Alliance Novices' Hurdle, Cheltenham, 16 March 1994

IN 1993 CHARLIE SWAN BECAME THE FIRST JUMP jockey in Irish racing history to ride 100 domestic winners in a calendar year. The same year he won the Ritz Club Trophy for leading rider at the Cheltenham National Hunt Festival, and repeated that feat in 1994. By the time he rode his tenth Festival winner on Urubande in the 1996 Sun Alliance Novices' Hurdle he was right at the top of the tree – one of the most popular and sought-after riders on either side of the Irish Sea.

Charlie Swan was born in County Tipperary on 20 January 1968, son of jockey and trainer Captain Donald Swan. By the age of ten he was riding in pony races, and at fifteen had his first winner under Rules on his first ride – in a two-year-old race on the Flat at Naas on 19 March 1983 on Final Assault, a horse owned by his grandmother, trained by his father and broken in by young Charlie Swan himself.

He went on to serve his apprenticeship with Kevin Prendergast at The Curragh, and rode fifty-six winners on the Flat before increasing weight dictated a switch to the jumps. So Swan joined trainer Dessie Hughes – who in his riding days had won the 1979 Champion Hurdle on Monksfield – and in no time was heading for the top. He was champion jump jockey in Ireland for the first time in 1989–90, and his fourth successive title in 1992–3 was won with a record total of winners: 104.

But it is the horses and races which count, and Swan has enjoyed great Cheltenham moments on such as Trapper John (1990 Stayers' Hurdle), Montelado (1993 Supreme Novices' Hurdle), Shuil Ar Aghaidh (1993 Stayers' Hurdle), Shawiya (1993 Triumph Hurdle) and Viking Flagship (1995 Queen Mother Champion Chase) in addition to big-race success on Cahervillahow (on whom, as well as winning several races, he was runner-up to Esha Ness in the 1993 'Race That Never Was' Grand National), Ebony Jane (1993 Irish National), Ushers Island (1994 Whitbread Gold Cup) and Life Of a Lord (1996 Whitbread).

His greatest moment – at Cheltenham or anywhere else – came on a horse who in the 1994 Sun Alliance Novices' Hurdle, the opening event on the second day of the Festival, was carrying the hopes, prayers and overdrafts of most of the Irish nation.

“I first rode Danoli in a maiden hurdle at Fairyhouse in November 1993, but I knew a great deal about the horse before then. He'd been bred just across the field from where I live in Tipperary, and I'd won races on a few of his half-brothers, so had always had a keen interest in the horse. Danoli had been unbeaten in three bumpers the season before, and his trainer Tom Foley was always confident that he'd make the top rank. Tom only trained a few horses and was very unused to being in the limelight: before his visit to Cheltenham in 1994 he'd never left Ireland!

As a ride, Danoli proved a bit of a character. Compact, not over-big, he wasn't what you'd call an easy horse. He tended to pull a fair bit, and although on the whole he was a good jumper, he'd occasionally take his mind off the job and step on a flight.

After winning those bumpers and making the transition to hurdles smoothly enough, winning his first two before running third when odds-on at the Leopardstown Christmas meeting, Danoli was building up a huge reputation in Ireland, and his performance in finishing a close runner-up to Fortune And Fame in the Irish Champion Hurdle in January 1994 made him look an outstanding novice. In mid-February I rode him in the Deloitte and Touche Hurdle at Leopardstown and he won very easily indeed from Coq Hardi Affair. Clearly he was spot-on for Cheltenham.

'He always pulls out a little more'

There was talk of going for the two-mile Supreme Novices' Hurdle on the opening day of the Festival rather than the Sun Alliance on the middle day, but eventually it was decided to aim at the longer race, and as Cheltenham got nearer the pressure started to build. On form Danoli was a good thing, an outstanding prospect, and during the weeks leading up to the Festival he was built up to be the Irish banker. I was very impressed with this horse and highly confident, but the nearer the race came the more I started to see why he might not pull it off: he'd never run over the distance of two miles five, the opposition was looking very stiff . . .

The more it became apparent that the Irish public were getting behind Danoli, the more my own optimism started to wane. I'd considered him a good thing, but then I was finding myself thinking: Why was I saying all this . . .?

There was, as usual, a big field – twenty-three runners – but Danoli was hot favourite at 7–4, with Josh Gifford's mare Brief Gale (who would return to Cheltenham to win the Sun Alliance Chase the following year) the only other runner at odds shorter than 10–1. All the newspapers were describing Danoli as the Irish banker of the meeting – *that* causes pressure! – and an additional turn of the screw was the fact that on the first day of the Festival the Irish had drawn a blank. Were Danoli not to produce the goods, depression would set in all round. But the punters' optimism seemed sky-high, and they cheered him as we cantered out past the stands. A great deal was riding on that horse that day.

Any anxiety you feel starts to disappear once you get up on the horse in the paddock, and by the time you're at the start you're just concentrating, as you would before any race, big or small, on doing your best.

With such a big field I had to be careful not to get too far behind and

157

risk interference when trying to make a forward move, so my plan had been to lay very handy – maybe third or fourth – and take it up late on. Danoli could pull like a train, but like many horses could idle in front, and I had to be careful not to expose him too soon.

In the event we were second or third down the back, and then climbing the hill he was going so well that I decided I had to let him go on. We hit the front at the top of the hill, the point furthest from the stands, and as we did so I could hear – even from that far away – a huge roar go up from the crowd. It was the Irish calling us home!

As we turned down towards the third last I knew that he'd keep going, as he always pulls out a little more. He jumped the third last well, a couple of lengths up on his pursuers, was still in the lead at the second last and hammered round the final bend into the straight full of running but with others lining up to challenge. The closest of these was Dorans Pride, but every time he got close to us Danoli would find a little more, and at the last flight we were still a length up, with Corrouge mounting a late challenge on the outer.

Danoli got in too close to the last and met it all wrong, but he was away from it so quickly that his momentum was hardly disturbed, and with Dorans Pride having fallen there and Corrouge breathing down our necks we set off up the final hill. I gave Danoli a few belts with the whip and he really stuck his head out, battling all the way to the line but never feeling in serious danger of being caught. We won by two lengths.

Dorans Pride (no. 7) is about to fall as Danoli flies far out over the last.

Sun Alliance Novices' Hurdle

Cheltenham, 16 March 1994   *2 miles 5 furlongs*

1 DANOLI	C. F. Swan	7–4 fav
2 Corrouge	C. Llewellyn	10–1
3 Brief Gale	D. Murphy	8–1

Also ran: Coq Hardi Affair (4th), Spring Marathon, What A Question, Empire Blue, Elaine Tully, Pondering, Mad Thyme, Hawaiian Youth, Divine Chance, Fine Thyne, Book Of Music, Man To Man, Strong Case, Le Ginno, River Lossie, Dorans Pride, Morceli, Tothewoods, Bay Mischief, Top Spin

23 ran   *2 lengths, 5 lengths*

It was a great performance by the horse and it triggered the most amazing scenes. All the way down the chute in front of the stands from the course to the unsaddling enclosure there were waves of Irish punters running down to the rail to cheer us in, and my immediate reaction was one of sheer relief that the Irish banker had come off – that it was all over!

We were mobbed all the way through the parade ring to the unsaddling area – scenes very reminiscent of Dawn Run's Gold Cup in 1986 and certainly the most fantastic reception I've ever known. Tom Foley was hoisted on to punters' shoulders, and it was impossible at that time to have even a brief conversation with him about how the race had gone. Amazing scenes!

Every Cheltenham winner brings a fantastic buzz, but this was very special indeed – and definitely the best experience of my riding life. **99**

Mark Dwyer

Forgive'N Forget in the Tote Cheltenham Gold Cup, Cheltenham, 14 March 1985

OF THE JUMP JOCKEYS HOLDING LICENCES AT the start of the 1996–7 season, four have scaled the twin peaks of Cheltenham by riding the winners of both Champion Hurdle and Gold Cup: Richard Dunwoody, Graham Bradley, Norman Williamson and Mark Dwyer. Of this quartet, only Dwyer can claim the added distinction of having ridden a Group winner on the Flat.

Mark Dwyer was born in Ashbourne, County Meath – an area steeped in racing history, not far from where Tom Dreaper trained Arkle – on 9 August 1963. He served his apprenticeship with trainer Liam Browne, and rode his first winner at the age of fifteen on 9 June 1979 at Limerick Junction (now Tipperary) on Cloneagh Emperor. He was champion apprentice in Ireland in 1981, the year he rode Dara Monarch to win the Group Three Anglesey Stakes at The Curragh at odds of 66–1.

Increasing weight caused him to switch from the Flat to jumps, and in October 1982 he moved to Malton to join trainer Jimmy FitzGerald: he got off the mark in England when winning a handicap hurdle at Market Rasen on Phoenix Prince on 16 October 1982.

It was his riding of Forgive'N Forget, who ran for six consecutive seasons at the Cheltenham Festival – landing a huge gamble in the Coral Golden Hurdle in 1983 and taking the Gold Cup in 1985 – which made Dwyer's name, and by the time he won a second Gold Cup on Jodami in 1993 he was in the top bracket of jump jockeys. The Champion Hurdle followed with the redoubtable Flakey Dove in 1994.

66 In terms of sheer ability there was very little between my Gold Cup winners Jodami and Forgive'N Forget, but Forgive'N Forget meant so much to me early in my career, and I was so closely involved with the horse, that the race of my life has to be his 1985 Cheltenham victory.

He was a horse I'd always followed quite closely. I was at Leopardstown when he won his bumper in 1982, and knowing that he had been moved to Jimmy FitzGerald's yard was an influential factor in my own decision to go there, as I knew that he'd be a good horse to ride. We always thought him a very good horse at home: he'd gallop with anything, six-furlong sprinter or two-mile stayer, and always come out on top, but he was very highly strung and had a mind of his own – his particular bogey was traffic – and not many of the lads wanted to get on him. Consequently I rode him out most days, and started to develop a close association with him which continued on the racecourse.

His 1982–3 season culminated in landing a big gamble in the Coral Golden Hurdle Final at the Cheltenham Festival, and he was back at the Festival the following year to run second to A Kinsman in the Sun Alliance Chase – which I had to sit out as I had dislocated my shoulder. With the Gold Cup the big target for the 1984–5 term, he was brought along gradually, picking up some good chases on the way, his final outing before Cheltenham being the Timeform Chase at Haydock: here he really had to knuckle down to beat By The Way after a great tussle from the last.

Jimmy FitzGerald is a master at getting a horse right for the big occasion, and going into the Gold Cup he was full of confidence. My own optimism had been slightly dented by Forgive'N Forget's having to work quite so hard to beat By The Way, but I knew that in a very open year – 1984 winner Burrough Hill Lad was forced to miss the race through injury – we had a serious chance.

Some had called Forgive'N Forget's temperament into question, but as far as I was concerned he was completely genuine. The key to him was that he was what I call a 'bridle horse' – he was a very good horse on the bridle but would not want to be off it for too long. He had a very high cruising speed and was always best when coming from off the pace in a strongly run race – which meant that the presence in the Gold Cup field of front-running novice Drumadowney would suit my fellow down to the ground. The plan was simple: drop him in and hold him up, and the stronger the pace the better he'd like it.

The weekend before the race Forgive'N Forget bruised a foot in training and was held up in his work for a few days, but I felt that this enforced rest would work in his favour, as he was always a better horse when fresh.

Combs Ditch was 4–1 favourite in a field of fifteen runners, Earls Brig second favourite, and Forgive'N Forget third market choice at 7 1, with two of Monica Dickinson's runners, Righthand Man and Wayward Lad, next in the betting, and another Dickinson horse, 1983 winner Bregawn, by then seriously in decline, out at 22–1.

It was pouring with rain by the time we got to the start, but the softening ground was working in Forgive'N Forget's favour. As we jumped off I kept him towards the back of the field, as the first priority was to get him settled and switched off – otherwise he would run too keen and waste his energy. By the time we had jumped the first two fences, passed the stands and headed off into the country, he had stopped fighting for his head and settled down into a perfect rhythm. Drumadowney was setting a strong pace but the rest of us knew that he was a top-notch novice and we could not let him get too far in front, so kept him well within our sights.

'As far as I was concerned he was completely genuine'

161

Tote Cheltenham Gold Cup

Cheltenham, 14 March 1985   *3¼ miles*

1	FORGIVE'N FORGET	M. Dwyer	7–1
2	Righthand Man	G. Bradley	15–2
3	Earls Brig	P. Tuck	13–2

Also ran: Drumadowney (4th), Half Free, Boreen Prince, Combs Ditch, Wayward Lad, Homeson, Door Latch, Ballinacurra Lad, Sointulla Boy, Bregawn, Rainbow Warrior, Greenwood Lad

15 ran   *1½ lengths, 2½ lengths*

Forgive'N Forget was taking his fences beautifully. He was a usually a good jumper but not what you'd call a natural – always careful rather than brave. As the race progressed his jumping got even better, and passing the stands after completing a circuit I was perfectly happy. He was coasting along, travelling very well indeed – and the better you're travelling, the longer you can wait to make your move. I knew I had everything covered and could see that nothing was going better than us. My only slight concern was how long Drumadowney would stay in the lead: I didn't want him to get too far away from us, but on the other hand could not let Forgive'N Forget get too far forward too soon.

By the water jump on the second circuit Drumadowney was coming back to us, with my fellow about eight lengths behind him back in sixth and jumping brilliantly. As we climbed the hill I pulled him out to go past a few tiring horses, then put him back towards the inner – and in no time he had moved into third behind Drumadowney and Half Free.

Forgive'N Forget was a horse who would get into gear very quickly, and coming down towards the third last he was running away. He jumped that fence still in third, and was on the bridle as we turned into the straight, where I asked him to quicken and get on the inside of Richard Linley on Half Free. He accelerated to take the inside berth but I still did not want him to hit the front yet; he missed the second last, which was very much in his favour, as it let Half Free get away and lead us for a little longer. Drumadowney started to fade and I went to the last on the bridle, then – ping! – he got three lengths with a wonderful jump and landed running. He quickened away from the fence and started off up the hill, and though he began to hang a little he was not stopping, and ran on with tremendous resolution to win by a length and a half from Righthand Man, who had made late progress without ever really looking like catching us.

I rode Forgive'N Forget in three more Gold Cups. In 1986 he again came to the last looking like the winner, but Jimmy FitzGerald's one specific riding instruction that year had been not to follow Dawn Run, who was known to be a dodgy jumper. Consequently I pulled wide up the straight as Jonjo and the mare went up the inner, and my fellow had too much daylight: he had a good look at the wing of the last fence and seemed to lose his concentration, but still ran a marvellous race – probably as good a race as when he'd won in 1985 – to come third behind Dawn Run and Wayward Lad.

A snow blizzard delayed the 1987 Gold Cup for an hour and a half. When we went down to the start for the first time Forgive'N Forget felt as good as ever, but after the delay he had completely lost his spark, and ran a flat race to come seventh behind The Thinker. Perhaps he was just too highly strung to be messed around in that way.

The 1988 Gold Cup brought the worst moment of my riding career. We were cruising along at the top of the hill behind Charter Party and Cavvies Clown, when something happened at the fourth last fence – I don't know whether it was on take-off or landing – and it was immediately apparent that he had damaged himself very badly behind. I pulled him up and dismounted, and having to stand there, holding this horse who had launched me on my career, waiting for the vet to come and knowing what his fate was going to be, was a nightmare. Perhaps it was in some way fitting that he should be dispatched on the course where he had enjoyed his most glorious moments, but it was none the less a tragic way for him to end.

Forgive'N Forget put me on the road. I'd ridden very little over fences in my first year in England, and it was my association with this horse over hurdles which led to my keeping the ride when he graduated to chasing.

I owe him a great deal. **99**

Forgive'N Forget with Half Free (centre) and Drumadowney at the second last.

Tommy Stack

Red Rum in the News of the World
Grand National, Aintree, 2 April 1977

Turf Trivia time. Which jockey rode Red Rum in most races? Not Brian Fletcher, whose twenty-seven outings on the great horse included the Grand Nationals of 1973 and 1974 (both of which he won) and 1975 (in which he was second to L'Escargot), but Tommy Stack, who rode Rummy in no fewer than forty-six of his one hundred races under National Hunt Rules, their ten victories together including the unparalleled third National win in 1977. And for good measure, Tommy Stack also spent a short period training the young Red Rum.

From a non-racing background, Tommy Stack was born in Moyvane, County Kerry, on 15 November 1945. He first worked as an insurance clerk in Dublin, but his interest in racing was kindled by his schoolfriend Barry Brogan, and after spending some time at the yard of Brogan's father Jimmy he decided to try to get into the sport. In 1965 he moved to England to join trainer Bobby Renton and started to ride as an amateur, his first victory coming in a handicap hurdle at Wetherby on 2 October 1965 on New Money.

After two years as an amateur Tommy Stack turned professional, and in 1971, on Renton's retirement, spent a short spell combining the roles of jockey and trainer – thus taking into his care the six-year-old Red Rum. Later that year he handed over the training reins to Anthony Gillam, and in 1974 became first jockey to the powerful stable of W. A. Stephenson. He was champion jump jockey for the first time in the 1974–5 season with eighty-two winners, repeating the feat two seasons later with ninety-seven.

Tommy Stack retired from the saddle in May 1978, soon after winning the Whitbread Gold Cup on Strombolus, to pursue a career in the Irish bloodstock world; then, in 1986, he took out a permit to train, his full licence coming in 1988. His effectiveness as a trainer under both codes was never better exemplified than in late April 1994, when he sent out the young chaser Gale Again to win a valuable race at Cheltenham, and less than twenty-four hours later landed his first English Classic with Las Meninas in the One Thousand Guineas.

The race of Tommy Stack's riding life brought a moment unique in racing history.

“ Red Rum arrived in Bobby Renton's yard as a three-year-old in 1968, by which time I'd been there a couple of years, and he was soon the apple of his trainer's eye – a very good-looking horse with a real presence to him.

My first ride on him in public was in a handicap hurdle at Cheltenham in September 1969, and I rode him over hurdles seven more times that season without winning: second place at Catterick and at Perth was the best we could manage. Early in the 1970–1 season we schooled him over fences, and his first session was dreadful: he scraped over the first of the little schooling fences, then refused at the second, a small open ditch! But when we got him to the racecourse for his first chase, a two-mile novices' event at Newcastle, he jumped from fence to fence and finished third.

This was the first time I appreciated one of his great qualities, which became even more noticeable as he got older and more experienced: he was a very agile, very athletic jumper, careful and efficient rather than spectacular – like a cat – and superbly balanced. Yet we didn't think him likely to make up into much more than a decent handicap chaser on the northern circuit.

After I gave up the struggle of trying to combine training and riding the yard was run by Anthony Gillam; then in August 1972 Red Rum was sent to the sales at Doncaster, where he was bought by Ginger McCain, who trained from behind his second-hand car business in Southport and who would work his horses on the local beach. I was at the sales that day and said to Ginger: if you buy that horse I'll ride him for you, but don't try to school him! I also suggested that working in the sea might help Red Rum's constant problem with his feet.

In the early part of that 1972–3 season we won three chases, and Ron Barry won another on him. Ginger was aiming Red Rum at the Grand National but my retainer with Newmarket trainer Tom Jones meant that I could not guarantee being able to ride him at Liverpool, and with Ron also unavailable for Rummy's next race, at Haydock Park in mid-November, Brian Fletcher was engaged.

By the time I next rode Red Rum, three years later, he had won two Grand Nationals and come second in a third, and was already one of the legends of racing. When Ginger decided to replace Brian Fletcher on the horse I was delighted to be offered the opportunity to renew our partnership, and although Ron Barry rode him in the 1975 Hennessy Gold Cup I was on him for the rest of his races that season, notably his fourth Grand National in 1976, in which we were narrowly beaten by Rag Trade.

Red Rum's 1976–7 season was geared towards the National, and for the fifth year in succession he came to Liverpool ready to run for his life – a great tribute to the way Ginger handled the horse. Rummy may have been a twelve-year-old by this stage, but he was as good as ever and was going into the National with a major chance. He was also, by then, a household name – the most famous racehorse in the land – and as his jockey I found the pressure starting to build: I was less worried about the niceties of tactics than about whether I'd fall off!

I was mightily relieved to get the build-up behind me and be legged up into the saddle, and Red Rum did his usual thing in the parade ring, bucking and kicking – he was always a playful sort of horse – and generally showing that he was on good terms with himself. As we paraded down past the stands he felt and looked more like a colt about to run in the Derby than a twelve-year-old gelding with over a hundred races under his belt, and then while circling at the start he started to give me the most wonderful feeling: he genuinely knew where he was, and this was *his* place – the king was in his kingdom. It was a remarkable feeling of self-confidence which in its turn put confidence into me.

There was a tremendous amount of public goodwill riding on him, though he was not market leader – that position went to Andy Pandy at 15–2. Red Rum and Gay Vulgan were joint second favourites at 9–1.

After a delayed start, caused by a demo about a convicted armed robber, we jumped off. As planned I found a line between the middle and outer, and took my time. Red Rum was never a horse who would run away, and from early in the race you'd need to be niggling at him a little to keep his position. Seven runners went at the first fence, and another four at the third – the big open ditch – and at the Canal Turn I couldn't believe there were so few horses around us.

Boom Docker, ridden by John Williams, had built up an enormous lead by the water jump – he seemed to be about a mile in front – but at the seventeenth, the first fence on the second circuit, he threw in the towel and refused, leaving the favourite Andy Pandy in the lead. We were in the chasing group, gradually moving up into second, and Red Rum was going wonderfully well. Andy Pandy was still well clear of us going to Becher's, and as he disappeared over the fence in front of us I heard the crowd roar: I knew he'd come down, but could not know where the fallen horse would be, and made an instant decision to swing to the outer. As we crossed the fence I could see Andy Pandy directly in front, so yanked Red Rum to the right, and yet again his wonderful balance proved our saviour.

This left him in front, with over a mile to go. He popped over the twenty-third, then going to the Canal Turn a loose horse came up our inside. I asked Red Rum to quicken to go past the loose horse, he jumped the fence, swung round and headed for home.

It was at this point that I started to become aware of the cheering – of the crowds lining the track roaring him home at every point. It was an exhilarating feeling, and from now on the race was simply a matter of keeping him going. As we crossed the Melling Road still in the lead and with nothing coming to challenge I sneaked a look behind. The only horse anywhere near us was Churchtown Boy, who had won the Topham Trophy over the National fences two days earlier and now seemed to be running away.

Coming towards the second last there were loose horses on either side of me, and I knew that Martin Blackshaw and Churchtown Boy were getting nearer and nearer. I eased back, saw a stride, and Red Rum jumped brilliantly. Then I heard a great crash behind me, and knew that Churchtown Boy had blundered.

One fence to go – Red Rum skipped over it and with the crowd going berserk he scampered off up the run-in, still accompanied by two loose horses. With the bedlam of cheering greeting his every stride, I couldn't help thinking about how Devon Loch had made his sensational slither in 1956 with the crowd similarly going mad, so pulled Red Rum clear of the inside rail, packed with people, and steered him round the Elbow four or five horses' width off the inner. He responded to the noise by sprinting through the final two hundred yards to finish, ears pricked, twenty-five lengths clear of Churchtown Boy – the first horse ever to win three Grand Nationals.

I'd never given him one crack with the whip at any stage of the race, and he felt as if he could go round again – he'd finished so full of running that on pulling up my first thought was to check that the weight-cloth was still there! It was an unbelievable feeling, and Ginger was understandably quite overcome: all he could say when he ran out to greet us was, 'Marvellous, bloody marvellous!'

The walk to the unsaddling enclosure between the two police horses went far too quickly. I was relieved that the race and all the pressure attaching to it was over, but I wish I'd been able to savour the immediate aftermath more. Winning the National was always my great riding ambition – the one race in my life I desperately wanted – and to land it in those circumstances

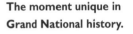

The moment unique in Grand National history.

News of the World Grand National

Aintree, 2 April 1977		$4\frac{1}{2}$ *miles*
1 RED RUM	T. Stack	9–1
2 Churchtown Boy	M. Blackshaw	20–1
3 Eyecatcher	C. Read	18–1

Also ran: The Pilgarlic (4th), Forest King, What A Buck, Happy Ranger, Carroll Street, Collingwood, Hidden Value, Saucy Belle, Zeta's Son, Davy Lad, Roman Bar, Pengrail, Andy Pandy, Prince Rock, War Bonnet, Winter Rain, Sir Garnet, Brown Admiral, Duffle Coat, Nereo, Sage Merlin, Castleruddery, Harban, Sebastian V, Royal Thrust, Burrator, Inycarra, Spittin Image, Willy What, Huperade, Gay Vulgan, Lord Of The Hills, The Songwriter, High Ken, Fort Vulgan, Boom Docker, Sandwilan, Foresail, Barony Fort

42 ran	*25 lengths, 6 lengths*

---

and in that manner on Red Rum, being part of something that had never been done before, was magical.

After racing we all repaired to the Bold Hotel in Southport – not far from Ginger's yard – for an almighty celebration, and late in the evening the hero of the day, Red Rum himself, was brought into the hotel – up the steps, through the foyer and along a red carpet into the ballroom – to take his bow. It was unbelievable how a horse could cope so calmly with that.

Red Rum was not able to return to Aintree for the 1978 race: he went lame a few days before and had to be withdrawn on the Friday. But he put the life back into the National at a time when it had fallen into the doldrums, for which all of racing is in his debt. **99**